VILLAGE TOURISM IN CHITWAN

VILLAGE TOURISM IN CHITWAN

Dr. Surendra Bhakta Pradhanang

ADROIT PUBLISHERS
Delhi-110 053

Published by
ADROIT PUBLISHERS
C-8/2, Yamuna Vihar, Delhi-110 053
Phone: 3266030, 3242552

Distributors
AKHIL BOOK DISTRIBUTORS
4675/21, Ganpati Bhawan, Ansari Road,
Darya Ganj, New Delhi-110 002
Phones : 3266030, 3242552
e-mail: akhilbooks@yahoo.com

ISBN : 81-87392-30-4

Layout by
Sudhir Kumar Vatsa

Laser Typeset by
Nidhi Laser Point
e-mail: nidhi_vatsa@hotmail.com

Printed in India on behalf of M/s Adroit Publishers by
Arpit Printographer, B-7, Saraswati Complex,
Subhash Chowk, Laxmi Nagar, Delhi-110 092

VILLAGE TOURISM CONCEPT
is
DEDICATED
to
MY NATION and WELWARE of PEOPLE
and
ABROAD

''घृणै गरोस मलाई गन्ध र कसिङ्गर सम्झी
तर, गन्धमै फल फल्न सकला
त्यो भोली नाना फल कहलाई!''

डा० सुरेन्द्र भक्त प्रधानाङ्ग, *फेरि के होला? १९७२*

*"Hate one thinking bad smell and wastage.
But, the fruit might grow even under the bad smell.
Tomorrow! that may be called a different fruit."*

Dr. Surendra Bhakta Pradhanang,
Pheri He Hola?, 1972

Preface

Village tourism in Chitwan is totally a new concept. It is the concept propounded at first by Dr. Surendra Bhakta Pradhanang of Nepal. At the outset, some tourism experts and big boss of tourism entrepreneurs do not like village tourism, because they thought that village tourism kills their tourism business and loose their monopoly power in tourism industry. Similarly, they do not like to share benefits derived from tourism to village and villagers. They consider village tourism is '*Sauta parryatan*' (rivalling tourism). Mostly tourism entrepreneurs who came from villages stayed in city, handled and profitted business and forget village and villagers' welfare. That is why they are concentrated to their own personal business and self-interest and self-protection. Despite of promoting village tourism, a group of tourism entrepreneurs misleading and joining hands with governmental authorities used to spread rumour like village tourism is a meaningless propaganda. But in fact it is a meaningful plan and proposition for the economic development of the nation especially villages and abroad. Gone are the days to hold tourism industry by a single powerful group of tourism enterprises. Today we need the balanced growth of tourism industry from hand to hand and from village to village.

Village tourism development in most of the developing countries like Nepal requires dynamic know-how. Most importantly, village tourism is a key factor of economic benefit to the tourism entrepreneurs and villagers living in Chitwan.

It concerns with man's activities with relation to villagers, mountains, valleys, wetlands, green forests, wildlife, climate and socio-cultural phenomena.

Village tourism is a planned and balanced industry. Its dimension is very broad. Benefits are shared by all in an equitable distribution pattern. Those who live in tourism regions are considered as participants in the tourism activities. Village tourism in which the villagers are not left as creatures but always graded as superior beings of their own circumstances. Above all, village tourism must address innovative transfers of technology, economic development and the socio-cultural environment. Village tourism is the best tourism among all types of tourism. It is above nature or eco-tourism.

Dr. Pradhanang who has been awarded with the title of 'Father of Village Tourism and Discoverer of Scientific Tourism,' contributed significantly to promote villages of Nepal. Now his idea proves that the ideal villages of Nepal are being able to cash in as best reward of village tourism.

Finally, village tourism in Chitwan which brings out the significant change in the village economy is an innovative strategy in developing tourism industry. It is beneficial to tourism entrepreneurs and people.

Kathmandu Research Centre
Kathmandu, Nepal

Acknowledgments

I am happy to be able to introduce the new concept of village tourism in the history of tourism industry in Nepal. I feel it has been my great success in my endeavour and research on tourism since the last several years. Village tourism which is a new experiment in enhancing Nepal's tourism industry has now been like a panacea for economic development of the nation. Today the marketing of village tourism is upgrading.

I would like to express my sincere thanks to Mr. Narayan Prashad Poudyal, Senior Ecologist DNPWC for supporting village tourism concept as a crying need of the nation especially for the upliftment of village economy and his valuable suggestions.

I appreciate the cooperation received from the Royal Chitwan National Park (RCNP), Kasara and Sauraha. Thanks are due to Mr. Gopal Prashad Upadhyaya, chief warden for his important informations.

My sincere gratitude goes to all inside and outside lodges, lodge owners, tourist guides, teachers, villages, local politicians, intellectuals, social leaders, professionals, lodge and hotel staff, Department of Taxation, Ministry of Culture, Tourism and Civil Aviation, National Planning Commission, Hotel Association, local NGOS, Hotel and Community Development Committee (HCDC) and tourists.

I indeed owe more thanks to Mr. Udaya Chandra Aryal, senior guide and chairman of HCDC who helped my mission with his valuable suggestions and informations. Similarly, he managed a favourable situation for contact with several tourists, lodge owners and lodge staffs without difficulties.

I also would like to thank Mr. Babu Ram Chapagai, guide and naturalist and Mr. Ram Chandra Ghimire, Member of Janakauli Village User Group, who assisted me with gathering villagers, village guides, tourism associated persons, naturalists and tourists and to take interviews and discussions smoothly. I sincerely extend my thanks to Mr. Basanta Mishra, the member of Nepal Tourism Board and proprietor of Temple Tiger Lodge for his positive support on developing village tourism concept.

I also express my special thanks and sincere gratitude to Mr. Rajendra Bantawa, president of Trekking agents Association of Nepal (TAAN) and Chairman of Great Himalayan Adventures (P.) Ltd. for his inspiring words and valuable support by organizing village based tourism programme, Trans-Himalayan 2000 on promoting village tourism in Nepal.

Finally, I thank the staffs of Kathmandu Research Centre for their assistance on the study of village tourism in Chitwan.

I fully hope that every tourism entrepreneur, villager, tourist and nation can be economically benefitted by enhancing village tourism.

Dr. Surendra Bhakta Pradhanang

September 15, 2001 Kha 1-533, New Baneswor,
Bhimshengola Kathmandu, Nepal
Telephone 9771-473019.
E-mail : drpradhanang@hotmail.com
Home page website : www.drpradhananghomestead.com

Contents

Map No. 1

NATIONAL PARKS, RESERVES, PROTECTED AREAS & PARKS AND PEOPLE PROJECT AREAS

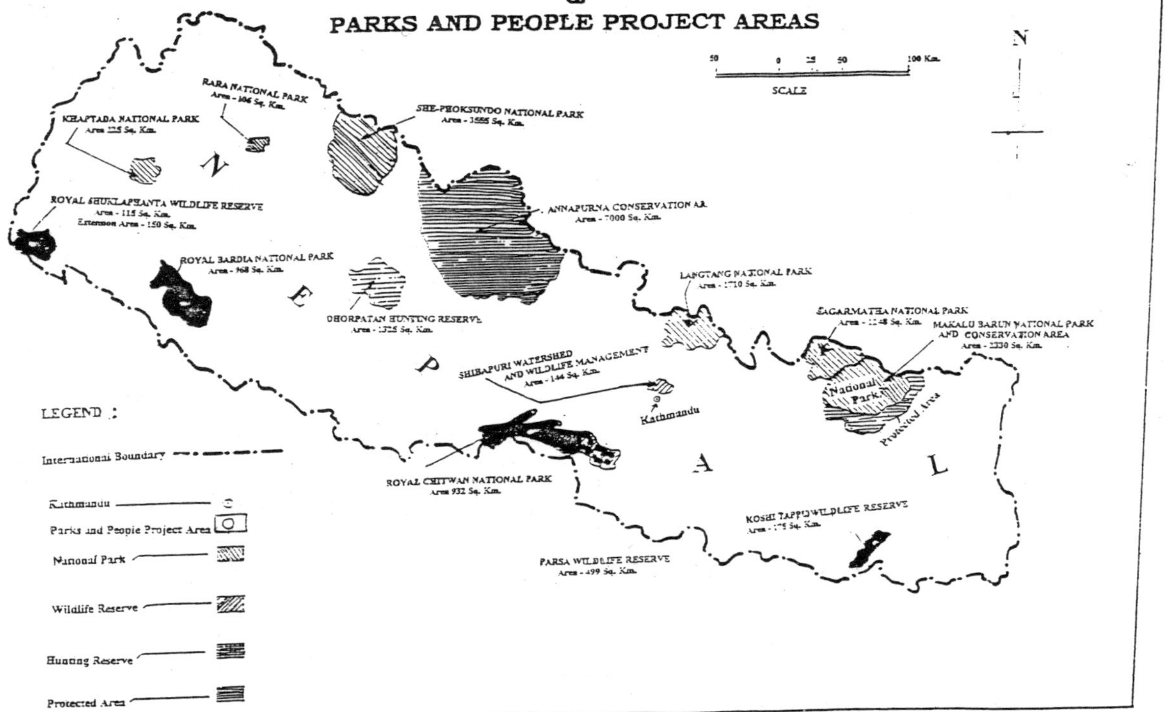

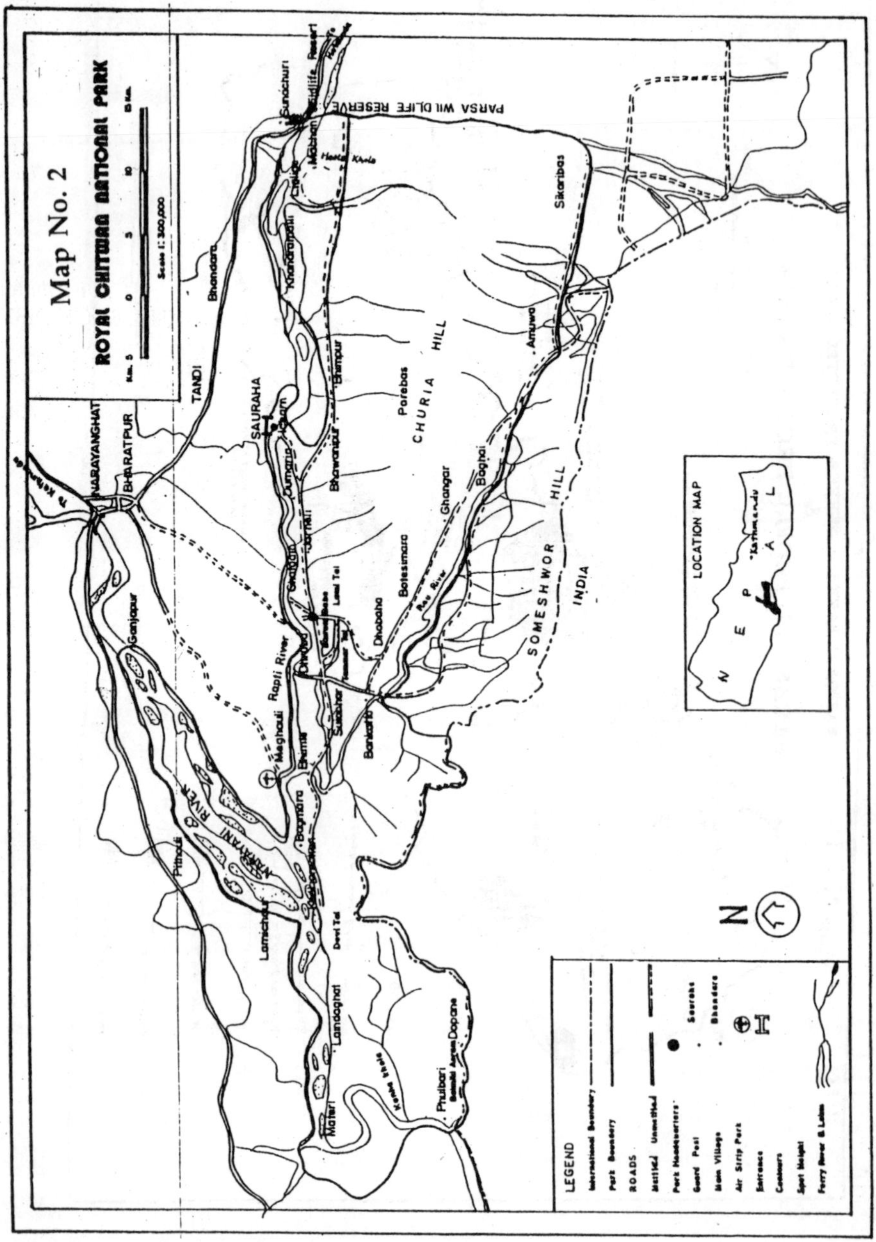
Map No. 2
ROYAL CHITWAN NATIONAL PARK
Scale 1: 300,000
NARAYANGHAT
BHARATPUR
TANDI
SAURAHA
Bhandara
PARSA WILDLIFE RESERVE
Rapti River
NARAYANI RIVER
CHURIA HILL
SOMESHWOR HILL
INDIA
Sikaribas
Amuwa
Meghauli
Ganjapur
Lamichaur
Laudaghat
LOCATION MAP
NEPAL
Kathmandu
LEGEND
N

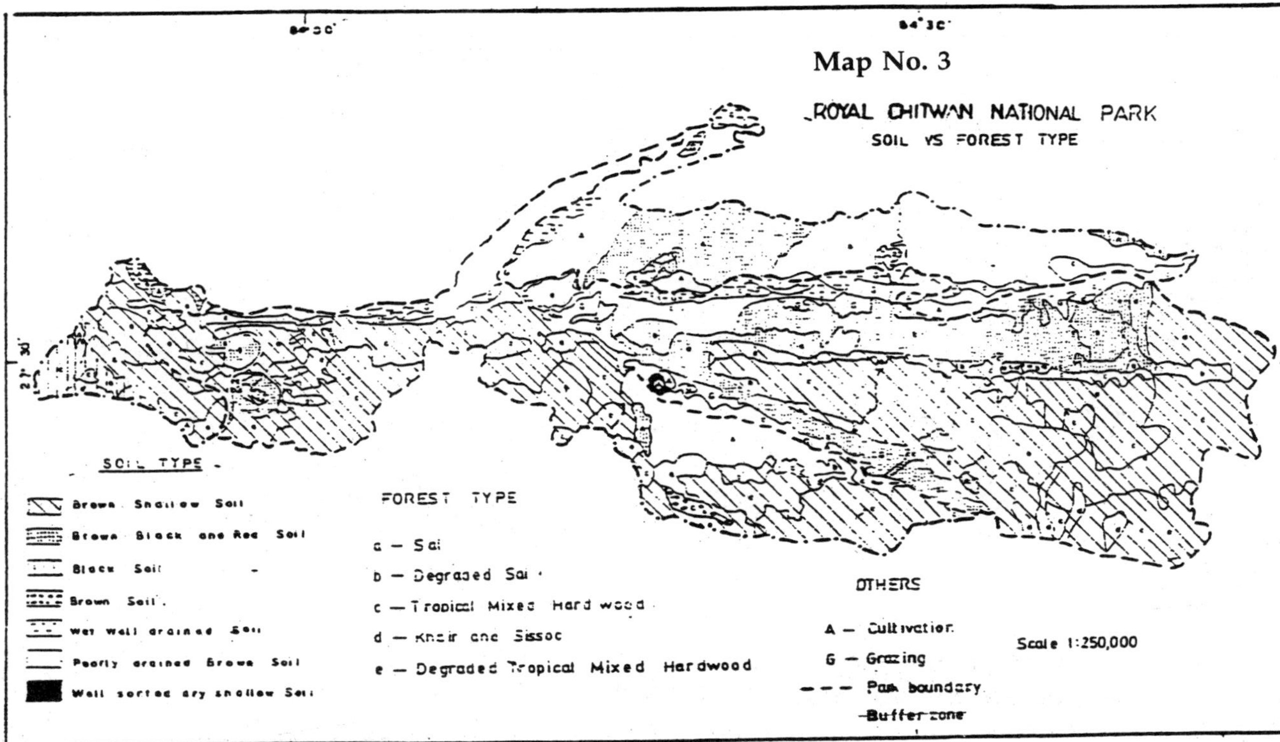
84°00'
84°30'
ROYAL CHITWAN NATIONAL PARK
SOIL VS FOREST TYPE
27°30'
SOIL TYPE
Brown Shallow Soil
Brown Black and Red Soil
Black Soil
Brown Soil
Wet well drained Soil
Poorly drained Brown Soil
Well sorted dry shallow Soil
FOREST TYPE
a — Sal
b — Degraded Sal
c — Tropical Mixed Hard wood
d — Khair and Sissoo
e — Degraded Tropical Mixed Hardwood
OTHERS
A — Cultivation
G — Grazing
Park boundary
Buffer zone
Scale 1:250,000

Map No. 3

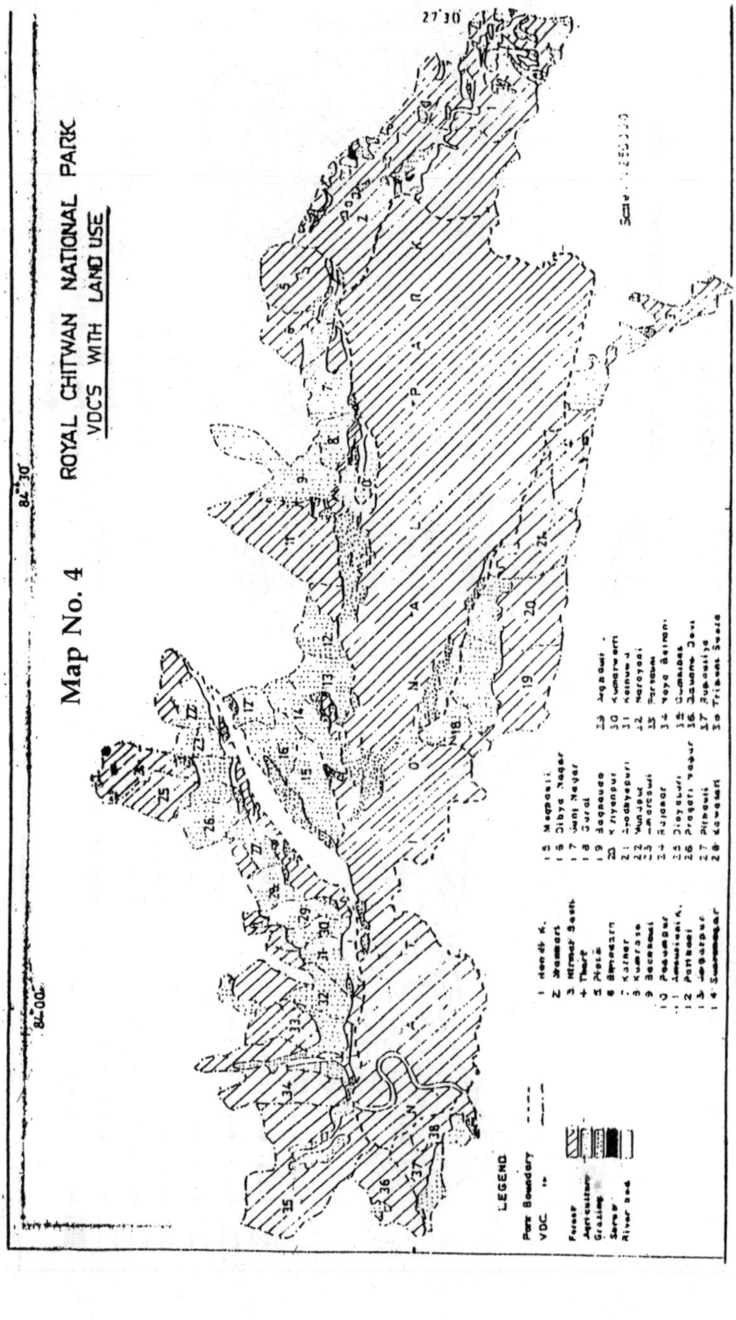
Map No. 4
ROYAL CHITWAN NATIONAL PARK
VDC'S WITH LAND USE
LEGEND
Park Boundary
VDC
Forest
Agriculture
Grazing
Scrub
River bed
84°00'
84°30'
27°30'

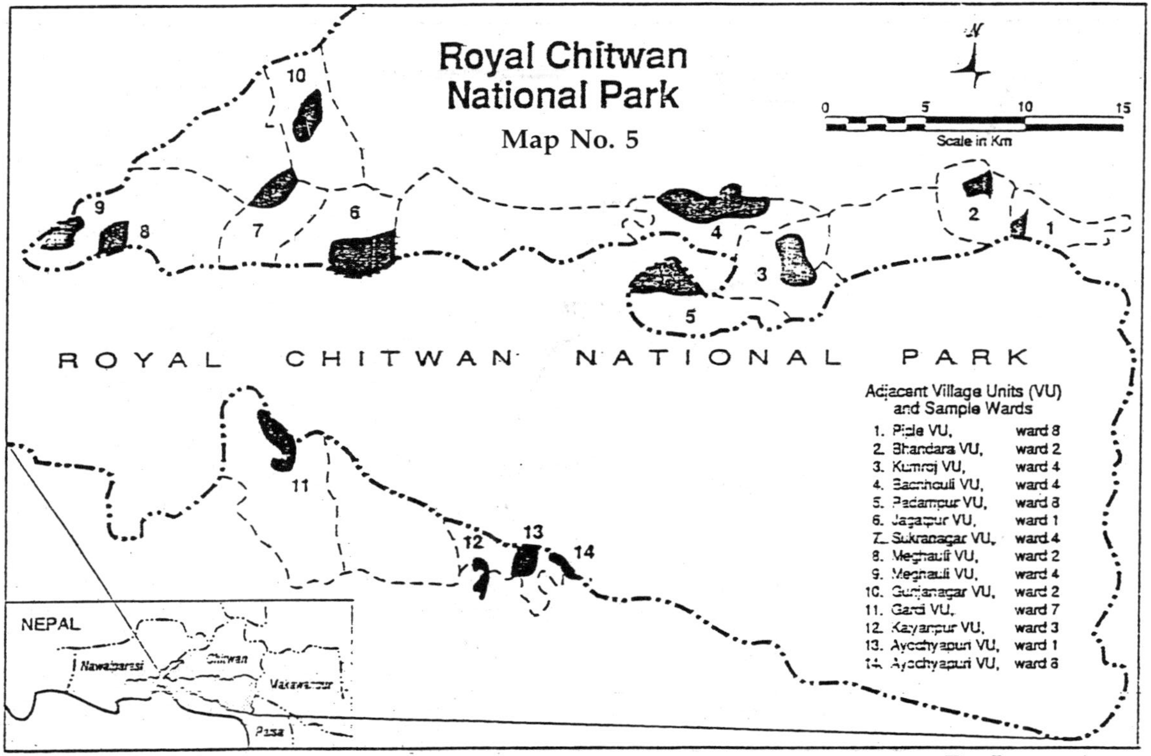

Royal Chitwan
National Park
Map No. 5
N
0 5 10 15
Scale in Km
ROYAL CHITWAN NATIONAL PARK
Adjacent Village Units (VU)
and Sample Wards
1. Piple VU, ward 8
2. Bhandara VU, ward 2
3. Kumroj VU, ward 4
4. Bachhauli VU, ward 4
5. Padampur VU, ward 8
6. Jagatpur VU, ward 1
7. Sukranagar VU, ward 4
8. Meghauli VU, ward 2
9. Meghauli VU, ward 4
10. Gunjanagar VU, ward 2
11. Gardi VU, ward 7
12. Kayanpur VU, ward 3
13. Ayodhyapuri VU, ward 1
14. Ayodhyapuri VU, ward 6
NEPAL
Nawalparasi
Chitwan
Makawanpur
Parsa

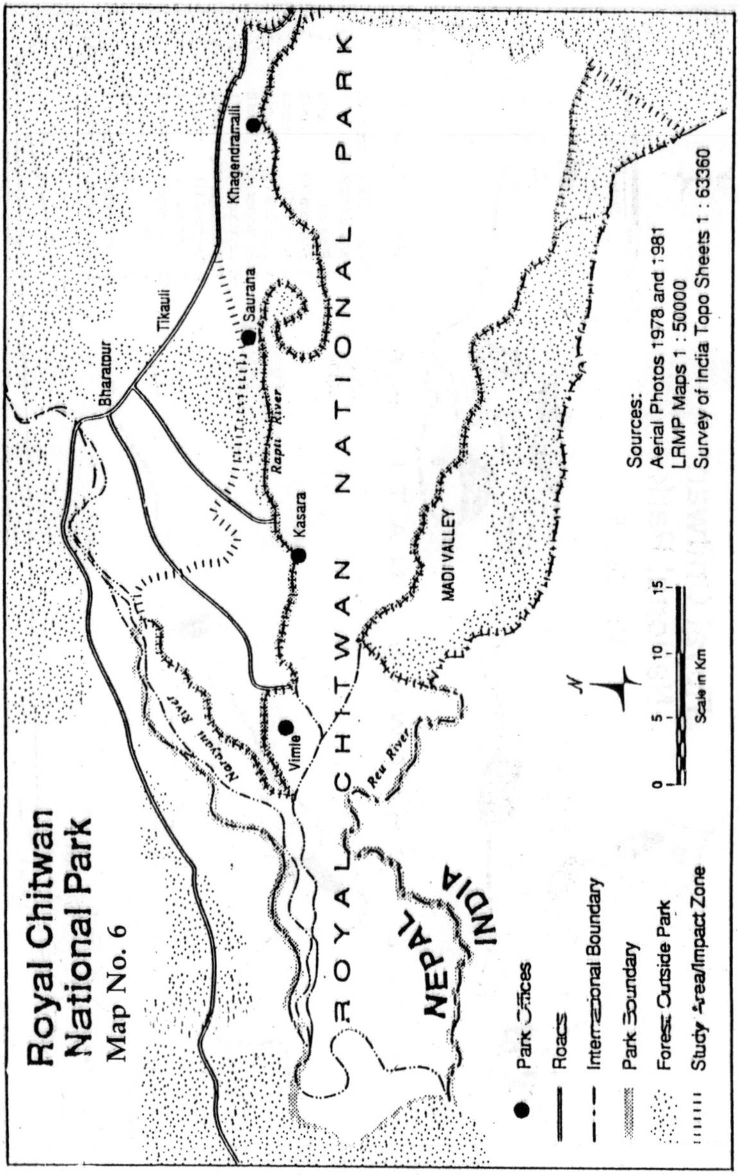
Royal Chitwan
National Park
Map No. 6
Bharatpur
Tikauli
Khagendramalli
Saurana
Kasara
Vimle
Rapti River
Narayani River
Reu River
MADI VALLEY
ROYAL CHITWAN NATIONAL PARK
NEPAL
INDIA
Park Offices
Roads
International Boundary
Park Boundary
Forest Outside Park
Study Area/Impact Zone
N
0 5 10 15
Scale in Km
Sources:
Aerial Photos 1978 and 1981
LRMP Maps 1 : 50000
Survey of India Topo Sheets 1 : 63360

Abbreviations

AD	=	Anno Dommini
ADB	=	Asia Development Bank
BS	=	Bikram Sambat
CBS	=	Central Bureau of Statistics
DNPWC	=	Department of National Parks & Wild Life Conservation
DOT	=	Department of Tourism
HA	=	Hotel Association
HCDC	=	Hotel and Community Development Committee
HMG	=	His Majesty's Government of Nepal
KMTNC	=	King Mahendra Trust for Nature Training Centre
KRC	=	Kathmandu Research Centre
NRs	=	Nepali Rupees
PP	=	Pages
RCNP	=	Royal Chitwan National Park
UNDP	=	United Nations Development Programme
VDC	=	Village Development Committee
WWF	=	World Wildlife Fund
TAAN	=	Trekking Agent Association of Nepal

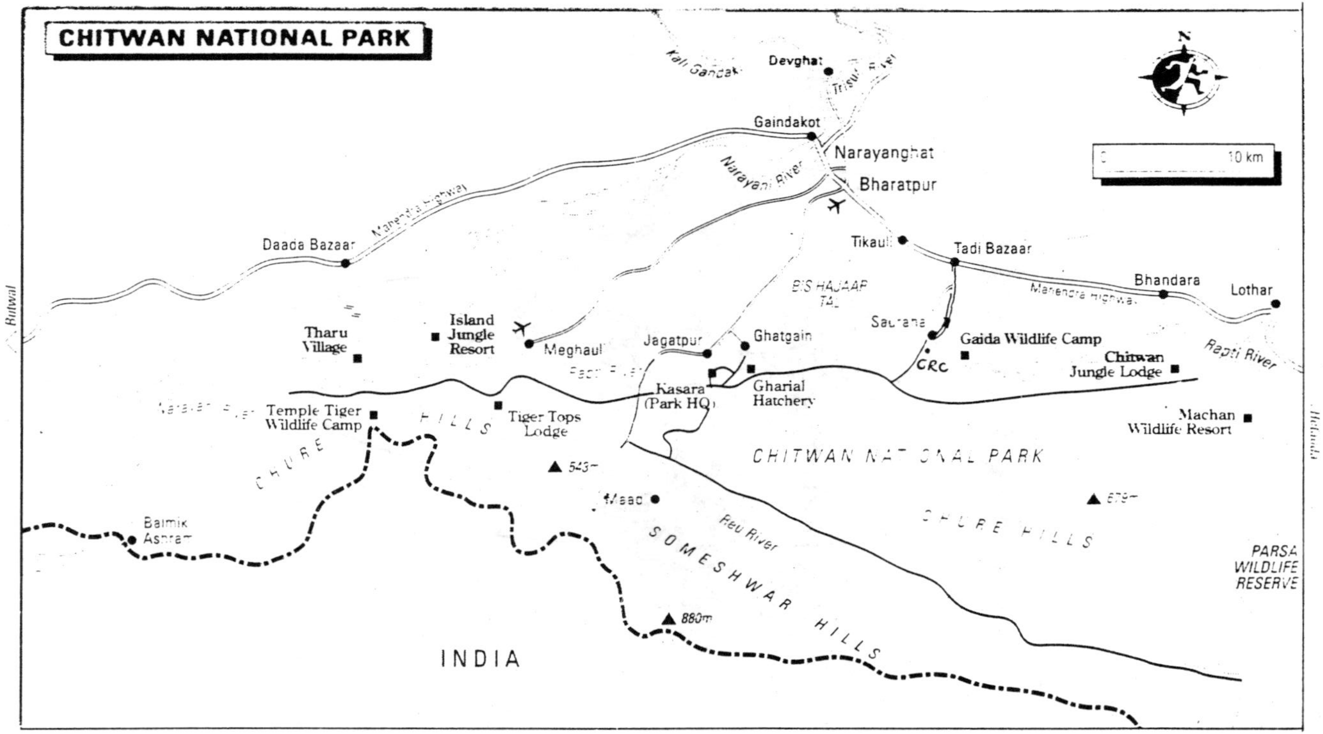
CHITWAN NATIONAL PARK
N
0
10 km
Devghat
Gaindakot
Narayanghat
Bharatpur
Narayani River
Mahendra Highway
Daada Bazaar
Tikauli
Tadi Bazaar
Bhandara
Lothar
BIS HAJAAR TAL
Sauraha
Gaida Wildlife Camp
CRC
Chitwan Jungle Lodge
Rapti River
Machan Wildlife Resort
Tharu Village
Island Jungle Resort
Meghauli
Jagatpur
Ghatgain
Kasara (Park HQ)
Gharial Hatchery
Temple Tiger Wildlife Camp
Tiger Tops Lodge
HILLS
CHURE
CHITWAN NATIONAL PARK
CHURE HILLS
PARSA WILDLIFE RESERVE
Maadi
Reu River
SOMESHWAR HILLS
880m
Balmik Ashram
INDIA
Butwal
Hetauda

गाउँ पर्यटन

1

INTRODUCTION

Village Tourism and Nepal's Tourism Economics

One who is going to look upon the world's best tourism site or accommodation centre should think about tourist village and village tourism. Accommodate small or micro to your mind and body. Small is comfortable and comfort in size. This writer who has been searching and researching the village and village tourism concept on the tiny principle since the last several years, defines tourist village and village tourism which can be a real tourism industry as the top business activity in the world. Nepal, in this circumstance, can lend the village tourism concept to the world. Nepal, being the country of Everest villages, can develop village tourism in its own designated style and originality. There is no longer a small world than a tourist village in Nepal. Nepal based village has its own special meaning and understanding.

Here small is easy to manage and understand. Small is good and small nation is further good. We achieve, when started working by small and small, the desired objectives. Nepal abounded by the beautiful land, reflects the microscopic vision, enlightening small is easy-busy.

The traditional tourist village philosophy provides many more nature and society based superluxurious boutiques and maximum utility service. Hence to cope with the competition, tourist village in small background can win the top list of demand for tourist accommodation or site in the world.

What is the defining characteristic behind a tourist village on the top of the tourism business or industry? To reply, the tourist village family, who pays respect and love to visitors, is a peculiarity of village tourism. Chitwan in this connection provides the best village hospitality service in conserved village and National Park.

Village tourism leads to dynamism in tourism industry. It concerns with all villages of Nepal. Most importantly, tourism in Nepal has been one of the most important supporting features of Nepalese economy. Tourism economics indicates the current foreign currency earning NRs 131.04 million which represents a 20.7 increase over 1996-97. Tourism contributed around 4 percent of the Gross Domestic Product (GDP) and 15.2 percent of the total foreign exchange earnings. In South Asia, Nepal lies in the fifth position by tourist arrivals and the third position by tourism foreign exchange earnings. The share of National Parks over foreign exchange earnings was recorded by 0.86 percent in 1998. The per capita, per day tourist expenditure was US $ 44.2. The total number of tourist arrivals was 89,834 in 1974 and 4,91,504 in 1999. The 'Visit Nepal Year 1998' could not be succeeded by evaluating tourist arrivals targeted by the government, average length of stay, foreign exchange earnings and volume of travel and tourism. By the fiscal year during 1974-75—1978-79, the five years mean average of tourist arrivals was 1,19,967. Similarly, during the period of 1989-90—1993-94 the five year mean average was 2,92,898.

Tourists visiting Royal Chitwan National Park (RCNP) were 836 in 1974-75 and 96,062 in 1996-97. The growth rate of tourist in 1996-97 was 14.49 percent. The five year mean average was 54,130 during 1989-90—1993-94. During 1974-75–1998-99 the tourist arrivals in RCNP are shown in Table 1.1.

Tourist arrivals by nationality in the National Park in order were USA (6639), UK (6101) and Japan (4173) (Table 6.4).

The revenue generated from the Park was recorded at NRs 27.15 million in 1991 and NRs 54.54 million in 1998. The growth rate was 13.27 percent. Out of the total revenue, the share of tourism was NRs 26.20 million in 1991 and NRs 53.12

TABLE 1.1

Tourist Arrivals in Nepal/Royal Chitwan National Park

Fiscal year	*Total No. of tourist arrivals in Nepal (i)*	*Percentage growth rate*	*Share of arrivals to RCNP by:*		*Percentage growth rate*
			Number (ii)	*Percentage*	
1974-75	90,431		836	0.92	—
1975-76	100,018	10.60	2,206	2.21	163.87
1976-77	103,870	3.90	5,021	4.83	127.60
1977-78	146,208	40.80	5,545	3.79	10.43
1978-79	159,308	9.00	8,325	5.23	50.13
5 yr mean Av.	**119,967**		**4,387**		
1979-80	164,380	3.20	6,290	3.83	- 24.44
1980-81	164,842	0.30	12,503	7.58	98.77
1981-82	165,943	0.70	11,218	6.76	10.27
1982-83	176,103	6.10	11,602	6.59	3.42
1983-84	186,522	5.90	11,774	6.31	1.48
5 yr mean Av.	**171,558**		**10,677**		
1984-85	164,546	- 11.80	14,606	8.88	24.25
1985-86	204,394	24.20	14,126	6.91	- 3.28
1986-87	238,361	16.00	25,490	10.69	80.44
1987-88	259,003	8.60	38,565	14.89	51.29
1988-89	248,453	- 410	44,896	18.07	16.41
5 yr mean Av.	**222,951**		**27,537**		
1989-90	246,361	- 0.80	N.A.		
1990-91	270,507	9.80	43,750	16.17	
1991-92	324,366	19.90	55,335	17.06	26.48
1992-93	306,286	- 5.60	58,442	19.08	5.61
1993-94	316,972	3.50	58,994	18.61	0.94
5 yr mean Av.	**292,898**		**54,130**		
1994-95	346,180	9.20	64,749	18.70	9.75
1995-96	380,301	9.9	83,898	22.06	29.75
1996-97	402,286	5.8	96,062	23.87	14.49
1997-98	440,283	9.4			
1998-99	4,77,774	8.5	105,880		

Source : (*i*) Nepal Tourism Statistics, 1998.
(*ii*) Royal Chitwan National Park, Kasara.

million in 1998. The growth rate in 1998 was 14.92 percent (Table 3.8).

Chitwan located at the middle part of Nepal stands at the altitude of 244 metres above sea level. It has spread in an area of 2519 sq. km. following Champaran, (Bihar) in south, Lothar, Makwanpur in east, Trihsuli river, Tanaku and Makwanpur in west and Trihsuli river Gorkha and Dhading boundary in north.

Chitwan, by name, is defined by the following three logical meanings; the place having plenty of Chital (leopard), 'Kuti' (forest hut), Balmiki Ashram—the platform of Sita and ruling land of king Chitrasen. To meet the third logic, the Tharu people are still worshipping Chitrasen in Chitrasari temple.

The Tharus live in plain land of Chitwan. Out of 15 castes, Rajput and Watar are known as Chitauniya Tharu (Tharu of Chitwan). The appearance of the Tharu originated from Rajasthan. Tharu is more or less similar to that of Mongolian. The Tharu men wear dhoti, kachhad, langoti, kamij and Chadar while the Tharu women wear changa, choliya, thenomi, sari and so on. The Tharu dresses are well designed in these modern days too. Tourists will prefer to buy more those dresses, if they are prepared and displayed beautifully as per the tourists' interest and demand.

There are so many important tourist spots such as Devghat, Balmiki Ashram, Royal Chitwan National Park, Bikram Baba, Upardang Gadhi, Someshwar, Chitrasri, Goddak, Bageswari, Shivaghat, Kabilas Gadhi, Purana Gadhi, Ichhaya Kamana, Kalikasthan, Bees Hazari Lake, Tribeni, Parshuram Kunda, Sivapanchayan temple etc. in Chitwan. Besides these, there is a beautiful hillock situated at forest area, Bharatpur ward No. 1. The picturesque of Chitwan can be witnessed and enjoyed from this spot. Apart from this, Jutpani Kalika, Hatiwang, Kandrang Gadhi and Lothar are virgin and unexplored pleasant places for tourism development in Chitwan.

Royal Chitwan National Park, covering 932 sq. km. South West of Kathmandu, is most probably, the best area in which to see jungle bio-diversity. The Chitwan valley is 100 Km. long from east to west and about 49 km. wide at its widest. It is mostly forested and has an average altitude of 190 metres. The highest point in the Park is about 815 metres in the Churia hills. The Park lies in the Chitwan district of the Terai at Longitude in 84°20'E and Latitude 27°30'N. The area is subtropical lowland bounded in the north by the Rapti river in the south by the Reu river and in west by the Narayani river.

The major vegetation is sal (Shorea robusta) and riverine trees and grasses. It consists of both tropical and subtropical fauna and flora. Regarding vegetation, it was estimated area covered by various habital types in RCNP. Table 1.2 exhibits the habitat types. Sal forest covers an area of 634 sq. km. that comes out to be 68 percent.

TABLE 1.2

Estimated Area covered by Various Habitat Types in RCNP, Nepal 1981-1983

Habitat Types	*Area (sq. km.)*	*Percent Area*
Sal forests	634	68
Grassland	138.8	15
Riverine forest	93.2	10
Riverbeds and water	65.2	7
Total	**932.2**	**100**

Source : Dhungel, 1985.

Besides, vegetation provides habit to one horned rhinoceros, tigers, clouded leopards, gaur bison, sloth, bears, sambhars, wild boars and elephants. The fauna consists of 43 species of mammals and 450 species of birds.

With regard to fragmented forest eco-system the elephants are freely wandering in jungle. A total of 25 elephants are residential and belong to the Parsa-Chitwan forest with occasional dispersal to the Bara-Rauthat districts. The conservation area especially the Churia Foothill forest can be a prime area for elephant conservation in Nepal. The tiger in Chitwan is a symbol of enormous power. In Chitwan alone, there is thirty-five breeding adult tigers. The Bengal tigers found in Nepal belong to the continent of Asia.

Monkeys known as 'Nepali Bandar' (rhesus macaque) live in the riverine forest and grassland in Chitwan. In the National Park, they are seemed very shy and smart. Some monkeys can be trained for enhancing village tourism as village tourism product.

The rhinos are plenty in and around the national park. This moment Chitwan has been known as a house of rhino, which is prefered by tourists. Undesirably, villagers are to stand whole night for the protection of crop from rhinos and other wildlife. In Sauraha, crop is damaged by wild animals. This loss can be compensated only by developing village tourism in villages of Chitwan.

Likewise, leopard known as panther or Chituwa are plenty in number in Chitwan. The Nepalese leopard has distinct identity. It is a solitary hunter and wonderful tree-climber. The gestation of the leopard can be entertained by tourists.

Chitwan is a paradise for bird watching to bird lovers and tourists. The appropriate periods can be scheduled at September-November and February-April when migrants arrive. More than 100 species of birds are seemed in Chitwan. For example, peafowl, jungle-fowl, parakeets, green pigeons, sunbirds, woodpeckers, ducks, and flycatchers, bulbuls. drongos, leaf warbles, babblers, allies, pipits, wagtails, swifts, swallows, bee-eaters, martins, nightjars, storks, herons, eagles, vultures, owls and so on are found.

By late April, winter birds would migrate whereas other birds would arrive for nesting. At the breeding time, the birds sing a song with sweet melodies. The birds like nightjars, owls and cuckoos used to sing song while at night. Male birds compete with other males for building mates as rivals for possession. Each female bird temporarily marrys with a male bird. But the female bird leaves her partner after laying eggs in search of a new one. Most of birds are monogamous throughout the season while the peacock and the baya weaver are polygynous. The nest built by the birds is cup-shaped or domed structure on a tree. The craftsmanship of nest is wonderful. Bays weavers would build a beautiful woven and retort-shaped design with vertical tubular gates. Some birds are annual migrants, travelled long distance from country to country as the international tourists. For instance, wintering ducks and wavers are identified as Trans-Himalayan migrants. But most of the birds are regional migrants.

The people living in Chitwan represent different ethnic groups of people who have different cultures. The Tharu, Darais, Botes, Kumales, Majhies and Chepangs are indigenous group of people. The RCNP has 37 Village Development Committees (VDCs).

Tharu and Tharu Culture :

The indigenous group of Tharu people is, it is claimed by the Tharu intellectuals, considered to be the ancestor of Lord Buddha. Now it has been proved by history that Gautam Buddha was Tharu recognised as one of indigeneous people

TABLE 1.3
Population of Tharu Tribe

Population	*Male*		*Female*	
	Number	*%*	*Number*	*%*
11,94,224	6,00,534	50.3	5,93,690	49.7

Source : CBS, 1991.

of Terai Nepal. He is also known as Shakyamuni belonging to Newar. Buddha's mother went to maiti (parent's house) for giving birth to a child. But, on the way, in Lumbini garden she gave birth to Siddharth Gautam. The Tharu having a long history spread in 23 districts of Nepal mainly in Terai. The total of Tharu population is approximately 12 lakhs exhibited in Table 1.3.

According to the Amarmati literature, during the period of ancient and medieval age, the Tharu settlement was widely spread in Nepal. The Tharu tribe by surname, is called Chaudhari. The centres for Tharu inhabitant located at Jhapa, Morang, Sunsari, Saptari, Udayapur, Siraha, Dhanusa, Mohatari, Sarlahi, Rautahat, Bara, Parsa, Chitwan,

Newalparasi, Rupandehi, Kapilvastu, Dang-Deukhuri, Banke, Bardiya, Surkhet, Kailali, Kanchanpur and Kathmandu valley are popular in Nepal. The Tharus have a rich culture followed

A composition of Tharu ornaments is given below :

Body organ			Name of ornaments
Tharu	Nepali	English	Explanation
Muri	Tauko	Head	*Magiya* : an ornament wearing in head by the Tharu and which is made of silver.
Kan	Kan	Ear	*Bir, Jhilmiliya & Tarki* : ornaments wearing in ears by the Tharu lady.
Nak	Nak	Nose	*Nathiya, Phorfi and Nathune* : ornaments wearing in nose by the Tharu lady.
Hath	Hat	Hand	*Agalabala, Legrahi, Pachhawala, Tariya, Bak, Bijaith, Josin* : ornaments wearing in hand.
Ghecha	Ghati	Neck	*Sutiya* (Katesiri), *Thosia, Chandra har, Taunk, Sikri, Hamel, Sikarhawa mala* : ornaments wearing in neck.
Goda	Khutta	Leg	Kara, Prira, dhuruwa, Bichhiya, Mundari : ornaments wearing in legs.
Math	Nidhar	Forehead	Tikli : Mark at the forehead with tika in a series of ornaments.

by a number of customs and manners. The Tharu group of people would wear a total of 32 different ornaments. The ornaments wore by Tharu lady from head to leg show the magnificent picturesque. The Tharu lady who stands on the traditional fashion will create the compassion and attraction. The Tharu male also wears an ornament named tarana in his ear.

The Tharu people prepare 100 different types of handicrafts such as mauni (a kind of bamboo), jal (neat), Chhatri (umbrella), doli (briddle carrying on long basket), Dhokila (vessel made of bamboo) Khatiya (bed), Chulo (furnance used for cooking), Hadi (pot made of soil) etc.

Festival

The Tharu festival is highly expensive. The Tharu people would spend a lot of money in celebrating a festival. Their economic conditions have gone down due to the high expenditure on observing festivals. In each and every festival, they enjoy a plenty of jad (a liquor made of fragmented rice) and raksi (liquor). The Tharus forget everything and reduce tension by playing *mandarak* (a kind of musical instrument) and drinking jad and raksi. The major festivals are—Maghe Samkranti, Dhureri, Gurahi, Chhutki, Dashiya, Sawan Samkranti, Hardhawa, Hareri, Pediya, Bagar Pujana, Chhath, Jurashital, Chauchan, Ghardekhwa, Shirwa Pawan, Ekadashi Vrat, Kudpawan Lawangi, Haraut (Basant Panchami) and Samachkewa.

Food :

The Tharus have a variety of dishes of cuisine. In festival, so many dishes of food are prepared that they could not consume all in a day. Next day they eat 'Basi Khana' (Stale food) more. Practically they have a popular culture for eating 'basi khana'.

The Tharu cuisines are : Tikari (curry), Mad (Soup made of rice), Bhatdhikwar (tightened rice), Amchur (pickle made of mango), Sirka (fruit juice), Sethaura (vitaminous sweet for women who get delivery), Chhahauda (a kind of spice), Bhakka (steam-rice-ball), Amot (processed mango product), Kasar (a kind of sweet ball), Ghonghi (a kind of insect used for food), jad (liquor made of fragmented rice), Daru (liquor), Sirki (dry vegetable), Sidhra (dry fish), Machhalar (fish), Aaluk Bharta (pickle made of potato and spices), Khichdi (watery rice), Khattimithi (a kind of pickle), Phulauri (a ball shaped fried bread) etc.

Song & Dance

The Tharus have their own distinct culture with beautiful

song and dance. The cultural programme celebrated each month as per the significance of season displayed by playing mandara. The popular dances of Tharu community are as : Jhumra, Birhain Chachar, Sakhiya (Badka Nach) (melody song and dance), Kathghori, Madhablala (Krishna-Radha dance), Gopichan, Latthi Nach (stick dance), Mungrahawa Nach (group dance), Banna Nach, Huradangwa Nach (Question-answer dwet song and dance), Daphap Nach, Mayoor Nach (Peacock dance), Tarawar Nach (Sword dance), Barmasa Nach, Jatajatin Nach, Mahira Devi, Hori Nach, Jharra Nach, Chor Khaliya, Raslila/Krishnilila, Saru Nach, Kathariya Nach, Bharthari Nach etc.

The musical instruments used by the Tharu community are madara, jhal, kastar, ghunghona, dappha, basiya, chiraiya latthi, chatapatiya baza, manjira and so on.

Games & Sports

Besides this, the popular Tharu sports are Chhur (Seasonal sport played in the months of January-February) ghodbasa, golikhelana, penk, gullidanda, basatika, lukisadha khelana, bakuriwala, murga ladai etc.

As the Tharu literature states that a century ago, there was a Tharu king named Raj Karingta who ruled over partially Nepal and India. The Tharu people claimed Raj Karingta was the ancient king of Tharu tribe. Besides, there were some other Tharu kings named Manik Parakhu, Tuidang, Ratanparakhu, Dangisharan, Manik Parakhu, Upardang, Chitdang, Madardang, Ugarsen, Saring, Bhajabraj, Dangwari, Jhusai, Harsinghdev, Suhijdev Tharu, Angar Dang, Muskdagav, Uransingh and Nadhav Singh in Nepal.

Once a year the Tharu people used to workship Marawak God for the protection from diseases and undesirable accidents during the month of Shrawan-Bhadra. Generally they have strong faith and belief in God.

TOURISM IN CHITWAN

Chitwan is well known as a major tourist destination. Long ago, Chitwan was a protected area. In 1946 B.S. the Rana prime minister, Jung Bahadur, protected the wildlife of Chitwan valley by monitoring a hunting reserve. The fall of the Rana dynasty resulted in new settlers, from the hills, in Chitwan's forest area. Now-a-days, the RCNP is both a tourist destination as well as a part of a Royal tour circuit. In 1962, Tiger Tops lodge, having 4 beds inside the RNCP, was started by Mr. Copeman, an American citizen. Presently the ownership of the lodge has been transferred to a British subject Mr. Edwards. Wildlife tourism is successful inside the National Park.

Tourists enjoy nature and wildlife species. The tourist standard lodges built inside the park are within a 12 sq. km. area. The service provided by lodges has been found to be

TABLE 1.4
Inside Tourism

Year	*Tourist arrivals*	*Per capita per day tourist expenditure US $*	*Average length of stay of tourists*
1996	27,500	116	2 nights/3 days

Source : Inside lodges, Chitwan

excellent. Here tourists are satisfied. In fact the RNCP inside tourism can be displayed as a model for high spending tourist. The seven lodges have revealed altogether about 1500 local direct employment opportunities (including employees on contract) and 600 indirect employment opportunities (including daily wages workers, plumbers, wood cutters etc.). The lodges earned a gross income of NRs 150 million in 1996. (Table 3.2). Per capita per day tourism expenditure was estimated at $116 as shown in the Table 1.4.

The number of tourist visiting inside lodges was recorded at 27,500 during 1996 (Table 1.4). The highest number of tourists visited Tiger Tops (7100) whereas the lowest number of tourist was recorded at Narayani Safari Camp (2000). The total royalty generated from inside tourism was NRs 9.7 million) (Table 3.5).

The top royalty payer (NRs 3 million) among the seven lodges was Tiger Tops. Royalty for forest (land) alone amounted to NRs 9.4 million (Table 3.5). Tax revenue

TABLE 1.5

Grading of Inside lodges by Standard and Facilities

Name of lodge	*Rating*
Tiger Tops	1
Temple Tiger	1
Gaida Wildlife Camp	2
Chitwan Jungle Lodge	2
Machan Wildlife Resort	2
Narayani Safari Camp	3
Island Jungle Resort	3

Source : Inside lodges, Chitwan

generated from inside lodges was NRs 5 million. Inside lodges were graded by standard and facilities. The first grade was scored by Tiger Tops and Temple Tiger, the second grade was scored by Gaida Wildlife Camp, Chitwan Jungle Lodge and Machan Wildlife Resort and the third position was placed by Narayani Safari Camp and Island Jungle Resort. (Table 1.5)

TABLE 1.6

Area Occupied by Inside Tourism

No. of lodges	*Occupied forest land in:*		*Capacity to use forest land in :*	
	Sq. Km.	*Percentage*	*Sq. Km.*	*Percentage*
7	84	9.01	848	90.98

Note : RNCP covers 932 sq. km. area.
Source : Sample Survey

The National Park can, therefore, be further utilised by 90.98%. It is stated in the Table 1.6.

Sauraha

Tourism in Sauraha was started in 1977 with a couple of lodges. Today the number of lodges has reached 53. The tourism pressure has increased within an area of 6 sq.km.

around the National Park (Interview taken with the National Park authority and the tourism related persons). In Sauraha more than 90% of the tourists visiting the national park were

TABLE 1.7

Tourist Expenditure Pattern in Sauraha During 1996

Item	*Expenditure (NRs.)*	*Expenditure ($)*
Food and beverage	1700	30
Accommodation	600	11
Sightseeing	100	2
Park recreation	2000	35
Miscellaneous	400	7
Total	4800	85

Notes : *(i)* The total tourist expenditure is for a night and three day package.

(ii) Per capita per day tourist expenditure, on average, is NRs. 1236 ($22)

(iii) Park recreation consists of park entrance fee, elephant ride, canoeing, bird watching, jungle walk and sightseeing.

(iv) The tourist expenditure data (Rs. 4800) represents peak season only. The tourist expenditure decreased to Rs. 1700 in the off-season.

(v) The exchange rate used was $1=NRs. 56.75.

(vi) The average length of stay was 3.8 days (KMTNC Report 1996).

Source : Sample Survey

local package tours managed by Kathmandu and Pokhara travel and trekking agencies. They were mostly of western nationality. The average cost or tariff of the package tours was $85 per tourist but the cut-throat competition among the lodges decreased this to $30 (generally in the off season). Per capita per day tourist expenditure (on average) during the tourist season was estimated at $22. It is depicted in Table 1.7.

TABLE 1.8
Tourist Arrivals in Sauraha

Year	*Tourist arrivals*	*Percentage growth rate*	*Dumping tourists (i)*		
			Number	*percentage of total*	*Percentage growth rate*
1992	29,921		1.795	6	
1993	29,497	– 1.41	2.065	7	15.04
1994	32,375	9.75	2,590	8	25.42
1995	41,949	29.57	3,775	9	45.75
1996	48,031	14.49	4,803	10	27.23
5 yr. mean avge.	36,355		3,006		

Notes : *(i)* A dumping tourist is a cheap tourist living on either unemployment or holiday fund.
(ii) Dumping tourists are estimated as per the survey.
(iii) Data available in the Fiscal Year 2049/50 B.S. was considered as the calendar year 1993 A.D.
(iv) Including Indian and Nepali tourists.

Source : Hotel Tatha Samudaik Samudaya, sample survey.

In 1996, the tourist arrivals in Sauraha were recorded at 48,031 and the average growth rate was 14.49%. The five years (1992-96) mean average was 36,355. The dumping tourists visiting Sauraha were 4,803 and the growth rate was 27.23%. The five years mean average was 3,006 (Table 1.8).

Out of the total tourist arrivals in Sauraha, package tourists (PT), locally managed, represented 70% of arrivals whereas Free Independent Tourist (FIT) arrivals accounted to 30%.

The local employment in outside lodges was 444 and the indirect employment was 100 (Table 3.3). The revenue generated from outside tourism was NRs 0.15 million (Table 3.4). The lodges earned a gross income of NRs 26.5 million (Table 3.3).

2

Tourism Entrepreneurs—The Key Actors in Nature Conservation in Nepal

Responsibility for Conservation

Nature conservation is today's hot cake laid in the bed of conflicts. The principle, we pursue, is to conserve the national parks and protected areas as a prime duty of each individual of the nation. Nepal is the home of majestic Royal Bengal tiger and the great one horned rhinoceros. It is the sanctuary recognized as the best habitat for rarest birds in the world. Nature conservation is, thus, a must. The bio-diversity of Nepal as compared to that of the world is very rich. It can be explained as follows :

TABLE 2.1

Bio-diversity Scenario

Name	*World*	*Nepal's Share in*	
		Number	Percentage
Plants	2,48,428	7000	2.8
Mammals	4,000	175	4.8
Birds	9,040	862	9.5
Reptiles	6,300	71 (141 suspected)	1.1 (2.2 suspec-
Amphibians	4,184	30	0.71 ted)

Source : SHEAC, Institute of Forestry, 1998.

Today's concern is to stress the importance of nature

conservation on the one hand, and the development of tourism on the other. Specifically, tourism entrepreneurs, either public or private sector, ought to be aware of nature conservation. Today tourism recognized as a backbone of national economy has almost been ranked as a number one industry in the world. We want tourism industry to be developed faster in growth rate, but not hesitate to forget conserving nature. There is a high correlation between nature conservation and tourism development. The prosperity, we have, in tourism is largely dependent on nature conservation. 'No environment, no tourism' is the message denoted to nature conservation. Life without conserving the nature will be turned like a barren land.

When we talk of Nepal's tourism industry which is generally concerned with the private sector. In fact, tourism in Nepal has already been privatised. Generally it has gone to the hands of private sector following a number of activities such as hotels, lodges, travel and trekking agencies, rafting services.

We think of conservation. Undesirably, it is considered as a sole government's job and liability. A very few people consider that conservation is our common responsibility. The National Parks and protected areas have been introduced with the objective of nature conservation in Nepal under the control of the Department of National Parks and Wildlife Conservation (DNPWC). The approach extended by the government in establishing network of national parks and wildlife reserves in protected areas is a way to conserve the nature while tourism development is the secondary job supporting the conservation for sustainable development. In that sense, it is not serious nor has given high priority to tourism development in Nepal. However, the National Parks have programmes to develop the nature based tourism or eco-tourism inside the park and its buffer zone. There are eight national parks and adjoining villages developed in our country where the new concept of village tourism has to start. For example, the Manaslu region was a restricted area in 1990. In 1991 it was opened for tourists. The government has adopted the environmental management plan for trekking and destinations in the area. Similarly tourism development has taken in Chitwan, Sagarmatha, Annapurna, Makalu, Langtang, Royal Bardia and so on.

The present status of tourism entrepreneurs and entrepreneurship in Nepal is basically lead by private sector. The national park and the government based tourism entrepreneur like Tara Gaun and UNDP funded project Quality Tourism and Park and People Project could not have effectively developed so far. Village tourism is successful in Sirubari of Syangja district and Tnulo Parsel Gaun and Kartike Deurali Gaun of Kavre district. The Nepal Tourism Board, the private and public partnership organization has come forward to enhance the national tourism industry. Although there are various tourism based government, non-government and private organizations in Nepal, tourism industry could not have successfully institutionalised. Individual influence and vested interest are being practiced uptill now.

The Ninth Plan has the policy and implementing strategy that environmental programmes which directly benefit the village people and which raise their living standards will be implemented with priority. The benefit of tourism should go to the village level. Thus , the local bodies in each development region are encouraged to develop a model tourist village.

National Park and Protected Areas : Concept

The concept of National Parks and reserves is known as "a generic term denoting and system of local tenure or zoning designed primarily to protect bio-geographical resources of nation or international importance and to preserve them in or restore them, to a region characterized by minimal human interference with natural processes" (*Allin, 1990 : 3*) National Park, I think, is a product of village tourism.

The national parks and protected areas should be free from all human exploitations. The concept of national park has originated from the establishment of Yellowstone National Park in the USA in 1872. Later on, most countries have followed the concept and importance of national park and protected areas. In the United States, public demand was created for recreational areas which have been known as the national parks and protected areas. Today the number of protected areas in the world increased to more than 3,000. In Nepal the national park and reserve management was taken from 1973 when the National Park and Wildlife Conservation Act 2029 was passed by the government. As per the provisions of the Act, DNPWC has a network of 8 National Parks, 4 Wildlife Reserves, 3 Conservation Areas, 1 Hunting Reserve including 5 Buffer Zone around national parks, covering the total area of 26,696 sq.km. (18.14%) of the country's total land (Table 2.3 & 2.4)

Tourism Entrepreneurs in and around the Royal Chitwan National Park

We need better environment to flourish tourism. Tourism is, thus, related with nature conservation and eco-system. The term, eco-system is concerned with both abiotic (air, soil, water, temperature etc.) and biotic components (plant and animals) which make a balanced environment. The environmental degradation caused by the change in physical, chemical, bio-chemical characters of air, water, land etc. threatens all the earth. So it is the great threat to mankind especially for tourism entrepreneurs pointing that not to disturb eco-system in nature.

When we talk of Nepal's national parks and protected areas of wildlife and nature conservation, it is necessary to score the name of the Royal Chitwan National Park (RCNP), the first National Park stood as model National Park in Nepal. The Chitwan valley recognized as a famous place for wildlife tourism in South Asia has a successful story of nature conservation. The park covering 932 sq. km. is located in Chitwan district of Narayani zone. In 1984 the Royal Chitwan National Park was declared a World Heritage site. In 1986 an area of 750 sq. km. adjoining villages was declared a buffer zone which consists of forests and private lands.

Tourists in the Protected Areas

Nepal's protected areas preferred by tourists have been the major destinations. Tourists enjoy wildlife Park, nature and culture. The highest number of tourists (105,880) visited

TABLE 2.2
Protected Areas in Nepal

Description	*Area in sq-km. (km2)*	*Year*	*Physiographic region*
Royal Chitwan National Park	932	1973	Terai-Sivalik
World Hearitage Site (WHS) 1994 Sagarmatha NP (WHS 1979)	1148	1976	High Mountain-High Himal
Royal Bardia NP	968	1976/1988	Terai-Sivalik
Makalu Barun NP	1500	1991	High Mountain-High Himal High Mountain-High Himal
Langtang NP	1710	1976	
Shey Phoksundo (WHS)	3555	1996	Middle-High Mountain
Rara NP	106	1976	High Mountain
Khapted NP	225	1984	Middle-High Mountain
Koshi Tappu Wildlife Reserve (WR) Ramsar Site 1987	175	1976	Terai
Royal Sukla Phanta (WR)	305	1976	Terai
Parsa (WR)	499	1984	Terai-Sivalik
Kanchanjunga Conservation Area (CA)	2035	1997	Middle Mountain-High Himal
Annapurna (CA)	7629	1992	Middle Mountain-High Himal
Manaslu (CA)	1663	1998	Middle-Mountain-High Himal
Shivapuri Watershed and WR	144	1984	Middle Mountain
Dhorpatan Hunting Reserve	1325	1987	Middle Mountain High Himal
Total		23919	

TABLE 2.3

Buffer Zone	*Area in sq.km.*	*Year*
Royal Chitwan National Park	750	1997
Royal Bardia National Park	328	1997
Langtang National Park	420	1998
Shey Phoksundo National Park	449	1998
Makula Barun National Park	830	1998
Total	2777	

Grand total (including PAS) 26696 (18.4%) of the country's total land.
Source :Department of National Parks and Wildlife Conservation, Annual Report 1998-99 (Shrawan 2055- Asadh 2056) p. 30.

TABLE 2.4
Tourist Arrivals in the Protected Areas

Parks/Reserves	*Foreigners*	*Indian*	*Nepali*	*Total*
1. Royal Chitwan National Park	55,518	21748	28614	105880
2. Royal Bardia National Park	2853	0	3011	5864
3. Langtang National Park	10889	0	0	10889
4. Rara National Park	144	4	0	148
5. Khaptad National Park	13	0	0	13
6. Royal Suklaphanta wildlife Reserve	159	59	578	696
7. Parsa Wildlife Reserve	2	0	332	334
8. Koshi Tappu Wildlife Reserve	446	1584	0	2050
9. Dhorpatan National Park	112	0	0	112
10. Shey Phoksundo National Park	489	0	0	489
11. Kanchanjunga Conservation Area	881	0	0	881
12. Sagarmatha National Park				21372
Total				1,48,317

Source : Department of National Parks and Wildlife Conservation, *Annual Report* 1998/99.

the RCNP and 21,372 tourists visited the Sagarmatha National Park in the fiscal year 1998/99. (Table 2.4).

Cost/Benefit Analysis

The cost/benefit ratio is very important in nature conservation with correlation to tourism industry. We should know the conservation cost on the one had and the

TABLE 2.5
Cost/Benefit Ratio

Name of Office	*Cost*	*Benefit*	*Cost-Benefit Ratio*
1. Royal Chitwan national Park	9521213	65043778	1:6.83
2. Royal Bardia National Park	6258377	6226068	1:0.99
3. Langtang National Park	5201764	3528779	1:0.67
4. Rara National Park	1975651	92495	1:0.04
5. Khaptad National Park	2692055	86960	1:0.03
6. Royal Suklaphanta Wildlife Reserve	4086940	982578	1:0.24
7. Parsa Wildlife Reserve	4101408	338989	1:0.08
8. Koshi Tappu Wildlife Reserve	2353759	1203523	1:0.51
9. Dhorpatan National Park	2635620	237507	1:0.09
10. Shey Phoksundo National Park	4329590	156994	1:0.03
11. Department of National Parks & Wildlife Conservation	101179144	20385715	1:2
12. Sagarmatha National Park	3558102	4206507	1:1.18

Note : Included social cost and benefit
Source : Sample Survey

conservation benefits on the other. The cost/benefit ratio ought to be calculated for strengthening nature conservation and tourism industry.

The Table 2.5 shows the cost/benefit ratio of the national parks and wildlife reserves in the fiscal year 1998/99. It has been found that the cost benefit ratio in the Royal Chitwan National Park and the Sagarmatha National Park is 1:6.83 and 1:1.18 respectively. The ratio includes social cost and benefit by conserving parks. The tourist visited in the RCNP was recorded at 10,5,880 and similarly in the Sagarmatha National Park was recorded of 21,372. The tourism revenue shared 97% in the total income of the RCNP. Tourism development in national parks is benefitted to nature conservation while heavy loss incurred in nature conservation without tourism development.

Further, the revenue (NRs. 89,599,893) earned by the national parks is more than the Annual budget (NRs. 83,978,000) estimated in the fiscal year 1998/99. The rest of the national parks and wildlife reserves where tourism could not have flourished, have carried out an economic burden like a white elephant to the country. The above data give message to us we need to promote tourism along with the nature conservation.

The derivation of secondary cost and benefit is a difficult task. The new values in terms of several primary benefits are as output associated with the expansion of economic activities of national parks. The activities, like the sale of merchandise goods, transportation, mobility of people, tourist flow etc. are the benefits increased to profits of trade and industry. The new profit and economic activities of firms and people are an example of forward linkage secondary benefit and induced or backward linkage secondary benefit. The employment generation is next benefit to the villagers and new wealth is generated. These benefits are taken as socio-economic or social benefit.

The national parks have a series of costs and benefits which are intangible. These intangibles are real terms in value but are taken under subjective judgement.

Entrepreneurs Collide with Resources in Parks

Tourism development in National Parks is highly income

elastic. But the conflict raised on lodge/hotel built inside and outside the national park is a big issue with regard to the nature conservation and its management. The complaints by the concerned lodge owners and nature related persons have strongly condemned as such.

2. Spread of pollution (noise, air, water and so on), deterioration of environment, disturbance to animals habitat, poaching, crowd in the park, practice of illegal activities etc. are supposed to be undertaken inside the park.
3. The sole or monopoly tourism business handling inside lodges is neither good nor socially justifiable.
4. The elephant and vehicle use by the lodge owners should be stopped. The elephant and bus service should be provided under the control of government.

Similarly there is a number of complaints by the tourism associated persons in Sauraha also.

1. Tourism business has been unscientifically taken in Sauraha where dumping tourism and dumping tourists are encouraged to practice. It has been next to Thamel which is popular in cheap destination. The environment damaged to wildlife and nature conservation decreases the charm of Chitwan. Consequently, the unfair business competition held by hoteliers spoils the tourism industry.
2. Disco and Western music entertained in Sauraha have badly hampered the Nepalese culture and wildlife environment.
3. The success of wildlife tourism inside the national park could not be witnessed by the ill-hearted people. The leg pulling habit formed in our attitude should be totally discouraged and above all the puller must be eliminated from the Nepalese Society.
4. Generally the outside lodge owners do not pay conservation fee nor tax revenue properly. So they have gone out of business ethics and have been the problem bearer in tourism industry.

Quest for Sustainable Tourism and Managerable Conservation

The conflicts, we feel, are not actual problems. They are just dissatisfaction of tourism entrepreneurs. Due to lack of management plan, the question of survival of the fittest is put in terms of issue.

Now we can derive the following guiding principles :

1. The management crisis in between nature conservation and tourism development should be removed. The better management plan eliminates all the problems and conflicts. Thus sound and scientific management strategy should be operated in this respect.
2. The lesson should be learned from the national park management plan followed by the Yellowstone Park of USA. Here is both nature conservation and tourism development taken inside the park. There is no question of inside and outside tourism in the park. But the main thing is nature conservation and tourism promotion that benefit all the people.
3. A code of conduct having strict rules and regulations is necessary to operate the national park and tourism. The grade of lodges quoting A,B,C and D should be provided on the basis of qualitative services. The dumping tourism has to be totally discouraged. At least US$ 120 per tourist per day expenditure should be fixed to accommodate the park.
4. The provision of secret and intelligence unit should be appointed to find out the illegal activities like poaching, declaration of environment, smuggling etc. The secret and intelligent agent should be very strong and powerful to watch the activities against the nature conservation and tourism law. The illegal work done by anyone else should be caught redhanded. A heavy fine be charged and the permit/license may be revoked. In this way we can control evil deeds.
5. The government is very poor in promoting tourism in Nepal. The Department of National Park and Wildlife

Conservation should provide equal priority to both nature conservation and tourism development. It is a blunder to consider that tourism in national parks is DNPWC's secondary job.

6. Environmental audit should be annually performed by the concerned authority. Basically, it can be operated into three categories :

   (a) Environmental final audit by government sector
   (b) Environmental internal audit by private sector
   (c) Environmental global audit by international organization.

   As per the environment reports, the nature conservation and tourism activities should be corrected. Environment and nature conservation, if deteriorated either by inside lodges or outside lodges, should voluntarily leave the park.
7. The monopolistic competition should not be allowed in the market economy. Today we need fair and perfect competitive market in the tourism business. Thus, no lodge owner should be a monopolist. There should be free entry or exit in the perfect market. But we should be obliged to pay respect to rules and regulations prescribed by the park and the concerned authority.
8. The government should be very active in conserving nature and promoting tourism. The plan and policy adopted by the government are better to be implemented honestly.
9 The carrying capacity by management in and around the national park should be calculated. The capacity of tourist destination and lodge is necessary to be fixed beforehand for planned tourism industry.
10. Animal-human conflict should be minimized by providing security measure and sufficient compensation fund for losses (crop damage, accident etc.) incurred to the villagers. The relationship has to be developed between them in terms of lovely and friendly nature.
11. Every lodge owner ought to conserve nature alongwith

tourism development. The villagers who are suffering from wildlife protection should be economically benefitted from tourism as a substitute. So village tourism is the appropriate strategy to develop in the buffer zone or park area adjoining villages. Thus, each lodge owner gaining benefit from the national park should distribute his income (atleast 10% profit) for social service such as village tourism development and its related economic activities.

Conserving nature is our prime responsibility along with tourism development in and around the national park. The government and tourism entrepreneur, following conservation policy strategy should neither be onesided nor biased. The principle we follow is "protect-use-benefit" the right way to nature conservation and tourism promotion with sustainability. Hence, we require a regular environmental audit emerged by National Park and Tourism Development Management Plan. The lesson should be learned from village tourism entrepreneurship and conservation management development in Sirubari tourist village.

Conclusion :

Besides this, the concluding notes prepared for nature conservation and tourism promotion are as follows :

1. We should pay respect to nature. Understandingly, respect to the nature means respect to God. Thus, we should not neglect the significance of nature.
2. Nature conservation should be tactfully operated by the enforcement of regulatory laws (bio-diversity conservation rule, forest conservation law, private forest nationalization act etc.) in the country.
3. The preventive measures should be followed with a set of programmes such as preparation of regular environmental reports, environmental awareness and so on.
4. Tourism activities change the environment and deteriorate the nature more or less. Thus, the tourism

entrepreneurs should preserve and restore the historic buildings, traditional houses, temples and mountains. None of entrepreneurs should go against the protection of nature, wildlife and forest conservation, archaeological and ancient tanks, ponds, rivers etc.

5. The national parks, wildlife parks, public parks and tourist villages shoald be promoted.
6. The government should conserve the nature and promote tourism together. The importance of tourism should not be minimized in comparison to nature conservation by DNPWC.
7. The concerned government authority should think of promoting community empowerment, village conservation funds, district conservation committees, resource conservation plans and public private partnership conservation programme, biotic management system and so on.
8. Sauraha Tourism Management Plan should be specially introduced and urgently implemented by the government to correct and bring out tourism in the right direction. The government's policy should be fixed and action oriented, but should not be frequently changed from dirty political influences.
9. Tourism entrepreneurs should totally leave the dumping tourism business which hampers Nepal's tourism industry. There should be no more room for the leg puller who tries to spread rumour against the village tourism industry.
10. The perfect competition in the market should be warmly welcomed while the monopoly in the market should be discarded.
11. Finally, to build a sustainable tourism business we must learn lessons we can better treat our earth

3

Tourism Impact Scenario

Village Society and Socio-economic Aspect

Tourism affects the village society and socio-economic patterns of the people. Tourists influence food habits, family structures, religion, language and psychology of the local people. They spend money while they stay for recreation in Chitwan. Actually, they create a chain reaction that produces additional economic benefit. They trade with various businesses that purchase goods and services locally or elsewhere. The business transaction is being operated through successive rounds of purchases. Consequently, the initial direct expenditure of visitors spreads and multiplies throughout the local and regional economy.

Tourism helps to keep local craft industries alive and saves the traditional weaving and wood carving. It generates, employment and income in several sectors of the economy as well as development of infrastructure and a number of industries. Tourism paves the way to total development of villages through generation of job opportunities and income. For example, tourism in Sauraha has brought the importance of output of land use by tourism and situational effect. Optionally, the output of land use (gross income) was NRs. 5,00,000 and output ratio between agriculture and tourism recorded 1:9.43. During 1972-76 the situational effect or increase of land value by tourism development was 1:40. It has shown in Table 3.1.

TABLE 3.1

Output of Land Use by Tourism and Situational Effect in Sauraha

Agricultural land use of 5 Kattha in NRs.		*Tourism land use of 5 Kattha in NRs.*		*Output ratio Agriculture: tourism*	*Situational effect of land value by tourism development*		*Land value ratio 1972 : 1997*
Input	*Output*	*Input*	*Output*		*Price/Kattha 1972 (NRs.)*	*Price/Kattha 1997 (NRs.)*	
26,500	53,000	3,82,800	500,000	1 : 9.43	5,000	2,00,000	1 : 40

Notes :

(*i*) Input on agriculture includes labour costs, fertiliser and insecticides.

(*ii*) Output from agriculture in one kattha of land consists of rice production (7.5 quintals). maize (3 quintals), musuro (50 kg.) and oil seed (tori) (50 kg.) per annum.

(*iii*) The local prices of rice per quintal (NRs. 800), maize per quintal (NRs. 800), oil per quintal (NRs. 2200) and musuro per quintal (NRs. 1100).

(*iv*) The agricultural land is supposed to be used for tourism development in Sauraha.

Source : Outside lodges, Chitwan

Tourism in Chitwan created income, employment and tax revenue to the nation and the local people. The total direct employment was recorded at 1944 (by combining inside and outside lodges). The total indirect employment was 6100. (Table 3.2 & 3.3).

TABLE 3.2

Local Employment and Income Generated from Inside Tourism

Year	*Direct local employment*	*Indirect local employment*	*Gross income of lodges (NRs. millions)*
1996	1500	6000	150

Note : Indirect employment consists of different seasonal employees on daily wages such as plumbers. labourers. Wood-cutters etc.

Source : Inside lodges, Chitwan

TABLE 3.3

Local Employment and Income in Hotel of Sauraha

Number of Hotels/ Lodges	*Number of direct employees*	*Average No. of direct employees*	*Number of indirect employees*	*Gross income of lodges (NRs. millions)*
53	444	8.4	100	26.5

Note : Indirect employment is related to supplies of milk, eggs, vegetables, plumber, labour etc.

Source : Hotel Tatha Samudaik Samudaya, Sauraha

The total tax respectively is exhibited in Tables 3.4 & 3.5.

TABLE 3.4

Tax Revenue Generated from Tourism in and around the Royal Chitwan National Park

Year	*Inside tax revenue (NRs. millions)*	*Outside tax revenue (NRs. millions)*	*Total tax revenue (NRs. millions)*
1996	5.00	0.15	5.15

Source : Department of Taxation

TABLE 3.5

Royalty Generated from Inside Tourism

Year	*Ele-phant*	*Vehi-cle*	*Boat*	*Elepha-nt gra-zing*	*Emplo-yee rene-wal*	*Lease payments*	*Total income (NRs. million)*
1996	34,000	27,500	20,500	68,000	1,50,000	94,00,000	9.70

Source : Inside lodges, Chitwan.

Tourism generated revenue of NRs. 53.12 million in 1998 (Table 3.8).

During the tourist season in 1996, different income generating tourism based activities such as clothing shops, book shops, curio shops and local bars operated in Sauraha.

TABLE 3.6

Tourism Based Economic Activities During the Tourist Season of 1996 at Sauraha

Tourism based Enterprises	*Unit*	*Monthly Gross Income NRs.*	*Monthly Gross Income as %*
Clothes shop	8	2,40,000	37.04
Book shop	3	45,000	6.94
Curio shop	3	63,000	9.72
Local bar	2	3,00,000	46.30
Total		6,48,000	100.00

Notes : *(i)* Clothes shop, book shop and curio shop have an average gross income of NRs. 1000/day. NRs. 500/day and NRs. 700/day respectively.

(ii) Clothes shop, book shop and curio shop are not purely involved in these particular goods but are involved in other commodities also.

(iii) Tourist season includes the months of October-December and February-April (six months).

(iv) Local, western style bars are run generally for 3 or 4 months only as a seasonal business in Sauraha. Each bar has an average gross income of NRs. 5,000/day.

(v) The figures quoted for income were obtained from the proprietors and are unaudited.

Source : Sample survey of business proprietors.

They earned a total gross income of NRs. 6,48,000 per month as exhibited in Table 3.6.

The monetary income (average income per household per month) generated from village based tourism in the project areas was indicated in Table 3.7.

TABLE 3.7

Income from Tourism in Different VDCs (Project area) in 1996

VDC	*No of houses surveyed*	*Percentage of houses affected*	*Average income per month ($)*
Bachhouli	179	22% (40/197)	60
Bhandara	137	2% (3/137)	40
Kathar	180	1% (2/180)	45
Khairahani	45	2% (1/45)	24
Kumrose	180	6% (11/180)	34
Pathimani	135	3% (4/135)	8
Piple	140	1% (1/140)	18
Total	996	6% (62/996)	50

Notes : (*i*) Average monthly household income was calculated by dividing total income (both direct and indirect) by number of houses that received monetary benefits from village based tourism. (houses affected by village based tourism).

(*ii*) Outside of the Bachhouli VDC, the privately owned tourism industry had virtually no impact on household income in the study area.

Source : National Conservation Research and Training Centre (NCRTC), 1996.

The multiplier effect indicates the additional spending or job creation caused by tourist expenditure. For instance income from the bicycle shops in Sauraha was NRs. 75,000 per month during the tourist season. (Table 3.9).

This is the multiplier effect. This effect is clearly seen as the transfer of money from one region to another as tourists travel.

TABLE 3.8

Revenue Generated from Royal Chitwan National Park

Year	*Total revenue (NRs. million)*	*Percentage growth rate*	*Share of tourism by*		
			Amount (NRs. million)	*Percentage*	*Percentage growth rate*
1991	27.15		26.20	96.5	
1992	39.68	46.15	38.29	96.5	46.14
1993	36.07	– 9.09	34.80	96.5	– 9.11
1994	41.52	15.10	40.07	96.5	15.14
1995	46.87	12.88	44.36	94.6	10.70
1996	48.29	3.02	47.01	97.3	5.97
6 years mean avge	39.93	11.34	38.46	96.3	18.76
1997	48.15	– 0.14	46.22	26.0	– 1.68
1998	54.54	13.27	53.12	97.4	14.92

Notes : (i) Data available in the fiscal year was considered as calendar year.

(ii) Fiscal year means July 16th-July 15th of the following year.

Source : RCNP, Kasara.

TABLE 3.9

Income from Bicycle Shop in Sauraha :

No of shops	*Average Gross income/NRs.*	*Total income per month. NRs.*
5	500	75,000

Notes : (i) Average income was calculated from the standpoint of peak (tourist) season only.

(ii) Bicycle are generally hired at the rate of Rs. 15/hour and Rs. 125/day during the tourist season.

(iii) Total income/month was calculated as the number of days x average income/day × number of shops.

Source : Sample Survey

But, tourism has some negative impacts, such as prostitution, gambling, drinking, smoking, drug addiction etc. The entrance of "hippies" dumped tourist and sex tourist damages the social culture. Similarly, a new generation is being influenced seriously. Tourism gives a cultural shock to the society and proves an antithesis to its promotion. It could shock local people with its waves of inflation. It disturbs geology. For example, the professional suppliers of souvenirs destroy rocks, carvings, paintings etc.

Tourism is, thus, a big source of income. It is a labour intensive industry followed by various types of labour force in different jobs.

Environmental Unit

Ecology is the science associated with organisms and the environment. The increase in tourism traffic indicates the loss of farmlands and natural environment. The Environmental impact is, thus, the outcome of man's activities including industrial and developmental works. There are so many causes deteriorating the environment such as local people's attitudes and activities, local development, growth of unplanned and uncontrolled tourism, poaching and several other illegal activities in Chitwan.

Basically, poverty is directly or indirectly related to environmental problems. We have a lack of an integrated approach between human ecology and protected areas. There is a rise in tension between the haves and the have-nots in Chitwan.

Today, preservation society is ecology and eco-system conscious. Conservation and preservation of natural resources have been the slogans of environmentalists.

A number of humanists, sociologists and NGOs have followed, as their mission, to make the public environmentally conscious.

Increasing construction in Chitwan causes great damage to the environment. The increase in the number of cemented houses in Sauraha show that the natural environment is being lost day by day. Sauraha had 53 lodges. Out of them, the number of nature based huts was estimated at 95 while the number of cemented houses and semi-cemented houses were estimated at 193. (Every lodge had 5 huts on an average). The nature based huts to semi-cemented house ratio was 1:2.03 as shown in Table 3.10. This demonstrates that tourism in Sauraha has deteriorated the natural environment.

We have a balanced environment in nature functioning eco-system as such.

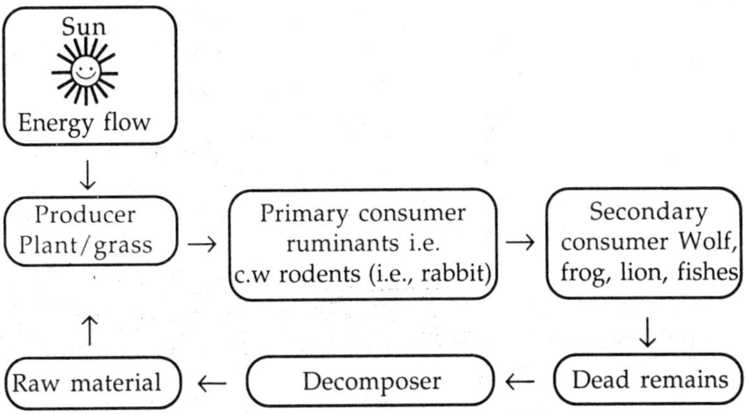

TABLE 3.10

Increase in the Number of Cemented Houses in Lodge/Hotel Construction

Year	*Nature based*	*Cemented house*	*Semi Cemented house*	*Hut : semi-cemented house ratio*
1996	95	5	193	1 : 2.03

Assumptions :

(*i*) A nature based hut is made of local materials.

(*ii*) A cemented house is a modern building made of cement.

(*iii*) A semi-cemented house is partially made of cement and the roof is riled or thatched.

Source : Sample Survey.

Several natural plant species were lost by unplanned and uncontrolled growth of new buildings. Similarly the number of elephant in the inside lodges was 68. Outside lodges used

10 elephants while the National Park possesses 40 elephants. (Table 3.11).

TABLE 3.11

Total Elephant in and around the RCNP 1996

Source	*Number of elephants*	*Percentage*
Inside lodges	68	57.63
Outside lodges	10	8.47
National park	40	33.90
Total	118	100

Source : RCNP and Lodges, Chitwan.

Generally, an elephant damages 4 sq.ft. of wild plants in the jungle with every step off-trail.

The vehicle run in the jungle numbered 55. They were mostly second hand vehicles in poor condition and produced much visible smoke emissions, carbon monoxide and sulphur in the park area (Table 3.12).

The total direct and indirect employment spread in Chitwan was 1944 and 6100 respectively. During 1996, 96,062 tourists (including India and Nepal) visited the park where the density was 103.04 per sq. km. The pressure of tourists was found to be increasing. Similarly, the population of Chitwan cannot be ignored. Heavy human use of open space adversely affects the bio-mass. Trampling directly kills wild plants. The expansion of a new tourist area changes the micro climate and water balance. It kills plants. Increased use of fuel-wood and timber loads leads to felling and cutting of trees. In the national park, 1,00,000 local people collected 12,000 metric tonnes of grasses such as Khar, Kharai, Phank, Baruwa, Babiyo and Simti per annum. (RCNP, 1996) An average lodge consumed over 13,000 kg. of fire-wood per annum. The annual fire-wood consumed by all lodges/hotels was about 4,52,000 kg.

Plants are also lost by plucking of wild flowers and leaves by wanderers. A number of rare plants in the jungle are being exhausted by tourists. Wildlife species are also badly affected by the proximity of man. The tourism phenomenon should

TABLE 3.12

Tourist Arrivals and Tourism Operational Units in Inside Tourism During 1996

Nature of lodges	*Local employ-ment*	*Tourist arri-vals*	*Ele-phant*	*Vehi-cle*	*Boat*	*Royalties from lease land forest (NRs. millions)*
Tiger Tops	375	7,100	16	12	10	3.00
Gaida Wildlife Camp	186	4,000	12	8	5	1.20
Chitwan Jungle Lodge	176	3,200	9	7	4	1.10
Temple Tiger Lodge	232	3,200	8	5	7	1.00
Machan Wildlife Resort	191	4,500	9	7	4	1.10
Narayani Safari Camp	206	2,000	7	12	5	1.00
Island Jungle Resort	134	3,500	7	4	6	1.00
Total	1500	27,000	68	55	41	9.40

Notes : Including employees on contract.
Source : Inside lodges, Chitwan.

not be turned into an antithesis to environmental ethics. Rather, it should be supporting action for ecological maintenance.

Geographically speaking, tourism is a landscape industry. Its products are made of natural heritage. The development of tourism is largely dependent on the significance and popularity of tourist sites.

Wild animals such as rhinos, died in the jungle due to natural as well as poaching. The Table 3.13 shows that during 1991-1996, 16 rhinos and 7 tigers died by poaching. Table 3.13 shows mortality record of rhino within RCNP.

TABLE 3.13
Mortality Record of Rhino within RCNP/Causes of Death

Year	*Natural*	*Poaching*	*Tiger kill*	*Total*
1991	7	1	1	9
1992	3	10	1	14
1993	7	4	4	15
1994	2	0	1	3
1095	6	1	0	7
1996	2	0	0	2

Status of the Tiger :

The results of Tiger census jointly conducted by DNPWC, KMTNC and Tiger Tops in 1995 show :

(i) A total of 107 tigers (27 adult female, 10 adult male and 70 sub-adult and cubs) has been estimated.

(ii) The average annual rate of increase was 2.6%. The census method applied was by means of a pug mark count.

Source : RCNP, Kasara.

The average garbage disposal per week was 5.3 drums during the tourist season and 1.6 drums during the non-tourist season. The size of the drums is 28 cu.ft. The total garbage disposal was 8 drums per hotel. Garbage and river pollution increased.

More than 96% of tourists told that lodges in Sauraha had already full capacity. The ecological impact assessment should be regularly done.

Tourist Carrying Capacity Building

Carrying capacity is very important to environmental protection and sustainable development. It is concerned with the maximum utilisation of any tourist site without having negative impacts on resources, visitor satisfaction, the community, economy and culture. Actually, carrying capacity cannot be easily quantified but its importance cannot be ignored with regard to environmental planning for village tourism and recreation.

Tourism carrying capacity consists of physical, biological, social and psychological components of the tourism environment. Mainly, three basic segments are categorised below :

1. Bio-physical (ecological) segment relating to the natural environment.
2. Socio-cultural segment relating to the host population and its culture.
3. Provision of facilities relating to visitor satisfaction.

Carrying capacity building changes as per the season, time, tourist behaviour, facility design and management, environment and attitudes of the host community.

4

Tourism and Planning in Chitwan

Background

Until 1950, the concept of tourism was unknown in Nepal. After 1950, Nepal opened its doors to foreigners. In 1956, Nepal established a Tourism Development Board under the control of the Department of Industry to develop the tourism industry throughout the country. In 1957 a separate Department of Tourism came into existence during the First Plan. Nepal prepared a Master Plan for the growth and development of tourism in 1972. The plan was concerned with various aspects like the economics of tourism, regional planning, a long-term perspective plan and an action oriented tourism programme. The master plan suggested five major potential areas for tourism development in Nepal. Chitwan was one of them.

The Eight Plan set five major tourism strategies. Out of these five, three major points were very important from the view-point of village based tourism. These were :

1. To expand the tourism industry and tourism activities which would help to ease poverty and raise the living standard of the population.
2. To promote environmental, historical and cultural heritage and raise the quality of services and facilities related to tourism.
3. To make efforts for the creation of stable development

within the tourism industry and link it to economic sector in a co-ordinated manner.

The prime objectives of the Ninth Plan show that tourism has been taken as the basic leading factor of poverty alleviation as well as the means of the overall economic development of the nation. A more liberal tourism policy will be undertaken to encourage domestic and foreign investors. Emphasis will be given to attracting more tourists and to encouraging them to spend more in the country by lengthening the average duration of their stay.

The Tourism Policy, 1995, has the policy and objectives to develop village tourism in Nepal. Emphasis has been given to the promotion of village based tourism. Besides, tourist activities will be extended in village in the basic of potential for tourism. During the Ninth Plan, fourteen tourism model villages will be promoted by facilitating tourist's needs and infrastructure. Every year, three villages, one from each ecological region, i.e. Terai region, hilly region and mountain region, will be implemented.

The Master plan for the Forestry sector 1988 states that it is important to facilitate and manage appropriate visitor use and tourism, as well as to bring economic benefit to Nepal without prejudicing material of cultural values. Further, it explains that every effort must be made to improve co-ordination in tourism planning.

The Seventh Plan set three major objectives to be taken. They were :

1. To meet the daily forest requirements of the people.
2. To maintain ecological balance.
3. To obtain the best possible economic returns from forest resources.

Further, the related policies and programmes to be implemented were highlighted as follows :

1. To mobilise people's participation in massive afforestation and forest conservation programmes in order to ensure supplies of essential forest products to the people.

2. To encourage forest farms to supply the domestic needs of forest products, provide raw materials for forest based industries and to produce industrial forest products.
3. To maintain established national parks, wildlife conservation parks and game reserves and to expand general and essential facilities as needed.

The Eighth Plan directed the augmentation of the supply and the reduction in the demand for forest resources. Private farm forestry was initiated with a view to increasing the supply of forest products.

The demand side shows that the conservation of eco-systems and genetic resources is an integral part of material resource management. Protected areas, particularly national parks and reserves and wildlife conservation areas contribute significantly with regard to bio-diversity, outdoor recreation and tourism in the country. Protected areas cover about 7.3% of the country. The government will preserve, promote and manage the conservation of eco-systems and genetic resources with the involvement of local people, so that they benefit from conservation rather than being alienated by it.

The Ninth Plan states that proper utilisation of forest resources will be undertaken with the prime objective of maintaining the balance between the eco-system and economic development. The productivity of land will be increased by programming forest oriented strategies. Emphasis on community forests, involvement of the private sector, research on forest conservation and herbs and the role of NGOs will be laid down in the plan. Giving priority to bio-diversity conservation, the tourism industry will be promoted through forest product development.

The 1993 amendment (2050 B.S.) of the National Parks and Wildlife Conservation Act, 2029 B.S. (1973 A.D.) has adopted the concept of a buffer zone. This amendment empowers any forested or agricultural area, including settlements, surrounding a national park or reserve as a buffer zone. A warden will be appointed as a powerful manager to manage the buffer zone. The act has the provision to spend

30-50% of the revenue generated from the park. A buffer zone can be divided into several components for management. The warden of the buffer zone will assist the different operational line agencies.

The village tourism Management Plan will be set up for five years with a twenty years term perspective scenario. The buffer zone around RCNP has several villages to promote. Chitwan consists of thirtyseven Village Development Committees (VDCs). (Figure 3)

Issues and Potential of Village Tourism

Tourism development is not an isolated task. It is inter-disciplinary work concerning different sectoral activities. The Chitwan valley is effectively lacking a tourism master plan.

Today, tourism in Chitwan is one way traffic mainly focused on the National Park. It has not really touched upon the buffer zone where several VDCs and villages are waiting for a village based tourism plan. They are waiting in the hope of getting benefit in lieu of their crops damaged by wild animals and the imposition of strict resource conservation rules. Conservation of the park does not mean suppressing the local people without allowing them to receive some benefits. There will always be a conflict between the park and local people as long as their annual losses due to crop damage go uncompensated. By developing some alternative sources of income to ensure their survival the problems can largely be alleviated. They complain that the lives of the wild animals within the National Park are rated higher than the lives of the local villages. In reality, it may be a problem for conservationists who will be responsible for village tourism development.

Lack of Tourism Priority

The Park Management policy has not given priority to village tourism. The concerned authority has been of the opinion for the last several years, that conservation is the primary concern and tourism should play a secondary role. It is for this reason that tourism control and management have been neglected. But, where the question of sustainability is concerned, we can lose the importance of money when we need income and capital.

Sustainability and income are as equally important as the two legs of a single person. "If he pays, it stays" is the principle of sustainability. We should leave the paradoxical policies. Conservation does not mean only protection. It means use and benefit by protecting. The old thoughts and policies should no longer exist while the concept of conservation has entirely changed. Hence, conservation without utilization is nothing.

No Assumption of Responsibility

Simultaneously, the local government, VDCs, NGOs and local administration seems to be unrelated and silent on the tourism development issue in Chitwan. The National Park, which is common property to all, lies in the Chitwan territory. The district administration and people are the concerned bodies who should not lose their liabilities. The local people and government are engaged in their own business. They pay no attention as if they have no concern with the National Park.

Lack of Tourism Regulation

Lodges have been built in Sauraha to the point where they are overflowing due to a lack of tourism regulations and the unplanned growth of lodges. In the market economy the price is determined by the two forces of supply and demand. But, the prevailing conditions are that the demand of tourists in Sauraha is low. Wildlife tourism should not be a cheap business characterised by low cost and discounted rates. "High cost tourists bring high benefits". In fact, high spending tourists are a boost to the national economy.

Entrance fee by nationality has no reasoning. The National Park charges NRs. 650 to international tourists and NRs. 10 to Indian tourists. The cost structure is highly discriminating. The park is visited by an increasingly large number of tourists but the park authorities still fail to provide basic information on the National Park.

Environmental Pollution by Industrialisation

The increase of industrialisation within Chitwan is a barrier to the promotion of tourism and it leads to the deterioration of the eco-system. Here, several factories producing, among other things, beer, paper, cement, iron and spirits have been the cause of environmental pollution. For instance, Bhrikuti Paper Mill has affected the western boundary of the National Park. The industry polluted the Rapti River and the Narayani River by the use of poisonous chemicals. The rivers are directly associated with canoeing. The pollution in the rivers creates a negative impact on water based recreation. In 1996, the water passing inside the park via the Narayani River was tested. The results showed a temperature rise of 1°C, salinity of 90%, a pH of 8.2, turbidity of 30cm. total phosphate content of 0.6 mg/l, a nitrate level of 0.1 mg/l, coliform bacteria uncountable/ 100ml. and the biological oxygen demand was 2 mg./l. Most of these are attributable to the paper mill. This statistical information has shown the growth of coliform bacteria and the increase in alkalinity in the Narayani River to lead to the destruction of aquatic life in the river.

Apart from this, there are other problems such as no provisions for compensation for injuries or losses sustained by contact with wild animals, lack of a code of conduct relating to villages, hotels, local government and the tourist and an absence of a positive relationship between the National Park and the local people.

All of these discussions, when combined together, explore some problematical questions :

1. Why has village tourism management not been planned at all so far as village development park conservation and people's benefit are concerned? Why has the conservation policy not been amended to reflect a more modern outlook?
2. Is an absence of village based tourism the cause of several issues to the national park and its adjoining villages? Can village based tourism play the role of an engine to power economic growth in the village of Chitwan?

3. Is there any ecological measurement that records the damage done by tourism activities in Chitwan? Why has the situation not been made clear by supporting statistical information? Similarly, have any steps been taken against the undesirable growth of industrialisation on the periphery of the National Park?

Potentials

Regarding the potentials of tourism in Chitwan the RCNP stands for wildlife recreation. The bio-diversity treasured within the National Park is world famous and is enjoyed by tourists from many countries. The park is a symbol of successful nature conservation in south Asia. It was Nepal's first national park, being established in 1973. The park has several interesting places like Kasara Durbar, the park headquarters, gharial breeding centre, Bikram Baba (religious site), Lamital, Devital, Chitwan Hatisar and the elephant breeding centre.

Chitwan has even brighter prospects for village tourism development of which are listed below :

1. Village Religious Tourism Sites

Chitwan has a very beautiful land mass of high archaeological and religious importance located at Dev Ghat on the banks of the Narayani River about 4 km. North west of Narayanghat. There is a rich riparian environment around Dev Ghat, it being surrounded by terrestrial forest vegetation. The Dev Ghat area has a deep significance and is a great attraction as a centre of village religious tourism.

The Balmiki Ashram in the Tribeni area of the south west of the park adjacent to the Indian boarder is a significant village religious site for Hindu pilgrims. Many people come to visit this place on the occasion of Maghe Aunsie. Similarly, more than 1,00,00 Hindu pilgrims come to Bikram Babu in the Kasara area, the park headquarters.

Madi is also interesting as a historical place. The site, known as Ayodhyapuri, is famous for punch Pandav's accommodation and travelling at the time of their twelve years jungle life.

Ethnic Culture

The community culture groups can be promoted as professional centres in Chitwan. The indigenous groups of people have a very rich culture. The world famous dances of the Tharu community can be identified as :

Lauro Nach (stick dance)
Damphu Nach (peacock feature bowing round dance)
Bhajeli Nach (big stick moving dance)
Bali Bhitrauni Nach (Harvesting dance)
Kartal Nach (wood clapping dance)

Similarly, the way of life and culture of other ethnic groups are equally interesting.

Community Forests

The community forests can be improved as green village tourism centres. Nature conservation is the prime objective of the national park management and with their support the local people can develop the buffer zone into a green belt of vegetation. The community forests, like the "ward ban" created in Swargadwari and Jagatpur can be developed as tourist village centres.

Extension of the Park and Tourism Activities

The National Park can be extended. For example, Beesh-Hazare lake can be promoted by planning village tourism and community forests.

Beesh-hazare lake is located in Gitanagar VDC at the Tikauli forest (Barandabhar) forest 5-7 km. south from the east-west highway. The prospect of the lake is more promising than that around of Phewa Tal in Pokhara. There are several types of aquatic plants such as phytoplanktons, zooplanktons and aquatic animals and birds. There are many kinds of animals namely crocodiles, gharials, fish, water fowl etc. in the lake. Ornithologists observe that the lake maintains an eco-balance and stable habitat for a large number of migratory and non-migratory bird species. It is very interesting to watch the birds activities in their natural habitats. This lake system will be a great attraction for tourists wanting to observe bird and animal species in the wild.

Concept of Village Tourism

Village tourism originated from Nepal is a new concept in the history of tourism. Nepal's village tourism which has its own peculiarity and originality is comparable to none. It is the outcome of a long research on tourism conducted by Kathmandu Research Centre. Village tourism, we have, is an innovative concept of Nepal and Nepali people prolonged for national development.

By definition, "village tourism is a grassroot level of tourism designated at its own Nepali village style, mobilized by Nepali people themselves, their skill and resources displayed as village life style and environment, involved by groups of village tourists, assigned by Nepali adult authorities positively within its balance of social and environmental function and strengthened the village and village economy" (Pradhanang, 1992).

In other words, village tourism is a common bridge in between domestic tourism and international tourism industry. In fact, it is an integrated approach on tourism development. Understandingly, village tourism is a major component of scientific tourism that creates the self-sustaining and self-standing economy. It is, in process a rooted tourism germinating its seed under the ground. To view the nature and complexity, village tourism is a non-foreign aid requiring concept.

Village for Developing Village Tourism

Chitwan based village has been illustratively identified. There are many magnificent villages, such as Bachhouli, Bhagaha, Janakauli, Meghauli, Telauli, Jagatpur and so on in Chitwan. These can all be promoted from the tourist view point of village tourism economics.

Sauraha

Under the Bachhouli VDC Ward number 2, Sauraha has

been a main tourist destination served by a large number of hotels. Many tourists stay here to enjoy nature and to see wildlife species. There is a visitor's centre and KMTNC office in Sauraha.

Bachhouli

Bachhouli village is a very interesting destination. It is located some fifteen minutes walk to the north-west of Sauraha.

The village is basically composed of Tharu people. It has 50 households occupied by 300 people. Here, tourists can enjoy observing the traditional lifestyle of the local people. Out of the total population, Tharu comprise 70% of the inhabitants while the remainder are Chhetri and Brahmin 20% and Gurung, Kami, Damai and Newar 10%. The education standard of the local people is low. They have only about a 30% literacy rate.

The Tharu ethnic group of people have an unusual way of welcoming guests. *Firstly*, they seat the guests on mats and then offer tobacco and water. *Finally*, they provide meat, fish and local raksi (spirits) to honour the guests. The women in Bachhauli are mostly very active using bicycles as their daily transport. The village is recommended as being suitable for a model tourist village.

Janakauli

Janakauli is an interesting destination, much loved by tourists. It is located east of Sauraha. The village comprises 129 households having a population of 774 people. The literacy rate of the locals is about 45%. The village has a mixed population of Tharu (65%), Gurung and Magar (20%), Newar and Brahmin (10%) and Kami and Damai (5%). It is here that Gaida Wildlife Camp specially conducts their village walk programmes. It takes about fifteen minutes to walk here from Sauraha. The main occupation of the village people is agriculture. The User Group earned NRs. 50,000 from the community forest project during the fiscal year 1995/96. The forest plantation was established on an area of 97 ha. of land.

Baghmara

Baghmara, which is located about 7 km. north-west of Sauraha, is a newly developed area located at Ward 3 in Bachhouli VDC. The area is dominated by Tamang people (80%) with the remainder being Brahmin, Chhetri and Damai. The population is about 1500 people who mostly follow agriculture. There is a view tower, having accommodation for four guests, in the community forest. Tourists can stay here to enjoy the wildlife having to pay $5 nightly. The KMTNC has launched several different community based programmes here. Community forest development has been very successful. The income generated from the community forest for the fiscal year 1995/96 was NRs. 0.79 million. While the local people used to benefit from community forest products, the emphasis has now shifted to its development as a mini-park centre.

Andrauli

Andrauli is a beautiful village, located in Meghauli VDC, Ward number 1. It is full of many local attractions such as the Shiva temple, Gaida lake (100 sq.m. area), Reu River, Rapti River and Narayani River. Canoeing and rafting, when properly managed, can be an attraction here. The population of 700 living in 100 homes makes this a particularly populous site having a variety of ethnic groups represented. The ward forest here is a model for community based forest development. The location of Swargadwari is an attractive site to watch rhino, deer and leopards.

Meghauli

Meghauli is a VDC comprising some 2027 households and having a population of 12,281. It is a heavily populated area of Chitwan having more than 32 villages. The literacy rate of the local people is only about 25%. Within the VDC there is the separate Meghauli village having 70 households located at Ward number 5. It is a Tharu dominated area. Since Meghauli is on the main route to Tiger Tops, several local Tharu people are employed there. It is accessible by road and air and sees a number of tourists who are *en route* to Tiger Tops.

Telauli

Telauli is a village in Meghauli VDC. It has a population of 450 of mixed ethnic origins (Tharu, Chhetri and Brahmin) living in 50 households. The literacy rate of the locals is about 40%. Their main source of income is agriculture. The village has two popular hotels, Chital Lodge and Rhino Resort. It is attractive for nature, wild animals and local culture. This village has a bright prospect of tourism development. The Rhino Resort constructed in tourist standard by providing different facilities in Telauli village area can be a village tourist hub centre for promoting villages of Meghauli VDC.

Bhagaha

Bhagaha is a village that is feasible to develop as a model tourist village. It lies in the Meghauli VDC and is situated in the buffer zone. It is an old and typically tiny village having about 45 households and a population of about 600. The indigenous Tharus, being only about 20% literacy rate, are very backward in education. The beauty of the village is enhanced by the Rapti River where tourists can go rafting or boating. This buffer zone site can be developed as a centre for bird and animal watching.

The lifestyle of the Tharu has its own special attractions that have been promoted worldwide. Tharu people of this village wear the traditional 32 types of silver and gold jewellery and make traditional handicrafts of bamboo and wood. Quality ropes are made here.

Jagatpur

Jagatpur is a beautiful VDC in an isolated spot on the bank of the Rapti River. It has 1493 households and a population of 7737. Here, can be seen the basic infrastructure of the Tamang community who lives on the western side of the VDC. The Indigenous ethnic group, the Kumale, also lives here. The local community forest handled by the User Group, is most effective being the home of many wild species like rhino, deer and bird species. The area can be developed similar to Baghmara in Bachhouli VDC. The people can get benefit from the forest and tourists can enjoy the beauty of the villages.

Village tourism can be developed to improve the local economy. The local community forest is an example of successful forest management. The plantation covers some 25 ha. of land.

Ghaila Lake, Kukur Lake, bird watching, cultural dance etc. are the major attractions to tourists. The local people, however, have a serious problem with crop destruction by rhinos.

Madi Kalyanpur

Madi is a small valley in the most remote rural area of Chitwan. It is located 12 km. south-east of Kasara at the Junction of four VDCs,—Gardi, Basantapur, Kalyani and Ayodhyapuri. It is in an area dominated by Tharu people. Historically, the Tharu migrated from Rajasthan to the jungles of Chitwan some 500 years ago.

Madi is a peaceful zone where the people are very honest and upright. It is surrounded by the Reu River in which was taken a bath by Pandav as in the course of time. On the Reu river beach tourism can be started.

Ayodhyapuri is famous as Pandav's dwelling place during their jungle life. Other attractions are Baikuntha Lake, Shiva temple, stone made boats, Pasram Kunda (pond), deep wells etc. In Madi, the people of this valley are destined to spend a hard life without having any basic needs. The prospect of tourism, however, is very bright if only we can develop the basic infrastructure.

The population of this valley is 6598 people living in 1238 households. The literacy rate is low at 20%. Here tourists can enjoy village life of the local people.

Kumrose

Kumrose is a very beautiful place located about 3 km. south-east of Sauraha. The population of the VDC is 6,443, who live in 1108 households. The literacy rate of the people is about 30%. The area is dominated by Tharu and Chaudhari people (70%) with the balance Brahmin and Chhetri (20%) and Damai, Newar etc. (10%). Agriculture is the main financial occupation with traditional fishing also being practiced. The latter will provide an attraction for tourists. The local handicrafts produced include Deli (a fishing basket) and Dhauka (fishing net). These will also be of interest to tourists.

Here, the community forest has been developed by the local people. KMTNC initiated various development programmes like bio-gas plants, vegetable production, seedling plantations etc. Gradually, tourists have been attracted to this area. Kumrose is important from the tourist point of view.

Bhandara

Bhandara is located about 10km. east of Sauraha and is connected by road with the highway. Here, basic infrastructure like roads, communications, drinking water and health services have been improved. Bhandara has a mixed ethnic group of people comprising Chhetri, Brahmin and Tharu. The population in Bhandara VDC is 10,424 living in 1975 households.

Wild animals can be watched in this area. Several historical sites as well as cultural and social activities can be seen here. The Tharu people present good attractions for tourists with their traditional dances. Sinchai Campital can be promoted as a Tharu cultural centre.

Village Based Tourism Model

Several villages adjoining the National Park can be developed as village tourism projects. Village tourism ought to be promoted by planning a short term as well as a long term (20 years) tourism strategy. Ecologically friendly communities or villages like Bachhouli and Bhagaha can be taken as tourism model villages through the active participation of User Groups and Functional Groups. The Tharu ethnic group of people, having cultural and natural beauties, attract tourists and village tourism. The human behaviour of local

The Tourism Village Multiplier Effect

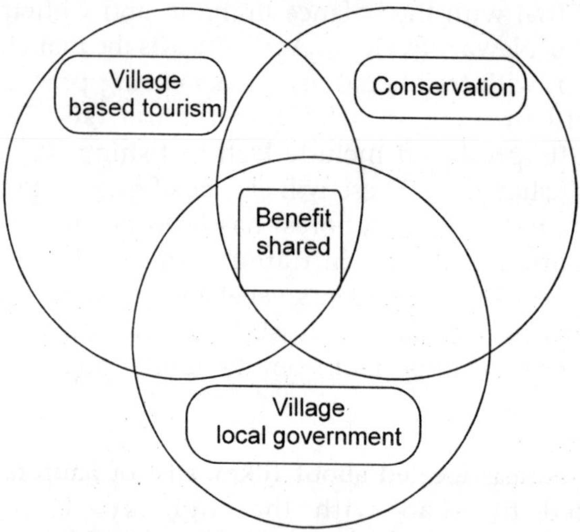

people is the preferred attraction of tourists alongwith park recreation. 55% of tourists visited Chitwan to enjoy wildlife as well as human behaviour as depicted in Table 4.1.

TABLE 4.1
Tourist Arrivals by Purpose of Visit

Purpose of visit	*Percentage*	*Total No. tourists surveyed*
Wildlife	35%	
Human behaviour	4%	102
Wildlife/Human behaviour	55%	
Other	6%	

Source : Sample Survey.

Village based tourism creates inter-relationship with chain reactions in the local economy. The figure below shows that every successive round of tourism expenditure creates a multiplier effect on the local economy.

Tourism Receiving and Giving Centre

The standard tourists in terms of high spending tourists categorising A and B class should be accommodated in Tourist Receiving and Giving Centre (TRG-Centre). They will be received with warm hospitality under the package tour programme preferably 3 night 4 days or more as per the tourists', interest and demand. Tourists would enjoy RCNP and unexplored Nepalese villages. The tourists will entertain with a number of nature and village based tourism programmes in co-ordination with Village Tourism Development Committee. The tourists who would take interest in village tourism will be guided and carried by the village guide and village tourism entrepreneurs.

Really speaking, tourists will enjoy with a special and specific test of village food and accommodation and above all the village environment. They can stay pleasant villages. They will be served with a traditional locally prepared food. The imported things are totally discouraged. The moment the village tourists stay village will naturally set free as nature paradise. The TRG-Centre is the inter-related and inter- communicated tourism centre in between village and city tourism development. It explains all about the village and significance of village tourism as a guidance with necessary informations. Such as brochures, visual aids and so on. In this respect, Rhino Resort recently built with tourist standard amenities in Meghauli village may be illustrated for village tourism promotion and village-city inter-relation.

Village Tourism in Favour of Promoting Trekking Tourism and Abroad

Village tourism as it stands now has an independent discipline by passing through various facets. The recognition paved as a planned industry that encourages indigenous traditions, art and culture. Nepal, being a land locked country, has a broader prospect for village tourism development with a series of land locked products such as rivers, mountains, Himalayas, lakes, villages, biodiversity, forests and so on. But, in this respect, Nepal should not remain as an idea locked country.

Village tourism is today's economic force that has been as a fertile land where every one can grow fruits, if dignity, equality and sincerity are wisefully considered. Village tourism which has a great economic and social power provides income concept and multiplier effect to every tourism entrepreneur and village and villager in terms of development of national economy. The nation covers villages and vice versa. By and large, we enhance our economic development pace village by village through the means of village tourism development concept. To develop tourism industry properly, there should be a good relationship between tourist and host population. Apart from this, village tourism has a brotherly relationship with Trekking tourism. Trekking tourism has been developed in Nepal since the late 1950. In fact, Trekking tourism has contributed more to Nepal's tourism development. It has a history of 50 years. The organised sector of Trekking Agents Association of Nepal (TAAN) has come to existence since the last 22 years. To institutionalise Trekking tourism in Nepal, TAAN has played a significant role. Trekking tourism designed in the last 50 years has been very old. Now is the time to modify the Trekking tourism with the collaboration of village tourism. The concept of village tourism has newly come up as the best of all tourism industry. Trekking tourism, though distinctly separated from village tourism, has to shake hand with each other. Trekking tourism can stay at different tourist villages to make trekking more interesting and enjoyable. Village tourism assists trekking tourism in every aspect of development with the supply of local food, drink, accommodation, culture, environment and so on. For example, a glass of 'village Mahi' is better than the imported coca cola.

The world tourist and tourism market has been attracted to village and village tourism. There is a wave come to village tourism development. As for an illustration, the village based international tourism event, Trans Himalaya 2000 was held in

Nepal with a grand success. The Nepali tourism village has gradually been today's E-village in the international tourism market. The programme boosted up village tourism from Kodari village to Janakpur village and the international media telecast the village scenario to the international tourism market. According to the study conducted by Kathmandu Research Centre, 60 percent tourist coming to Nepal would like to visit and stay at village of Nepal. The tourism market trend is towards the villages rather then the city. Tourists do not prefer to stay in city and Kathmandu due to degraded environment and pollution. Now the tourism market is basically concentrated to villages. Trekking tourism, in this situation, can promote its tourism business activity smoothly. To stand a good chance, Trekking tourism should be modified with a series of village tourism programmes in different trekking routes. The new trekking routes alongwith village tourism development should be added as a new product. Trekking tourism can nicely be promoted to more than double if village tourism and Trekking tourism go together with partnership. Trekking tourism lead by 24.3 percent is the statistical data of 1998. This can be reached to 60 percent by developing village tourism on the one hand and by modifying Trekking tourism in Nepal on the other.

In fact, developing village tourism is developing Trekking tourism and developing Trekking tourism is developing village tourism. They are interrelated with each other. Besides this, village tourism promotes city tourism, Kathmandu tourism and above all, the national tourism with a series of village-city communicated tourism development activities and abroad.

Tourism coming to Nepal are dumped tourists by 25 percent in total tourists arrivals. By nature the dumping tourists who want excellent facilities with low cost are being increased. The tourists, who want to spend US $ 100 per day, are just spending US $ 9 per day due to the dumping tourism business badly operated in the name of tourism development. Their average length of stay in Nepal is 20 days. As Kathmandu Research Centre suggested to revitalize Nepalese tourism policy and warned to face the danger of dumping tourist inflow to the national economy.

Today we need to create the sound environment for tourist expenditure as a mere demand for boosting tourism economy. The money US $ 91 saved by tourism market that can be insulated by village tourism development concept. Village tourism is thus, a challenging concept which promotes the national tourism industry as a whole in every aspect of promoting tourism activity.

Information to Trekkers and Mountainers

Today trekking and mountaineering, being the adventure based job, is popular in Nepal and abroad. Trekkers and mountainers, when climbed mountains, are frequently suffered from high attitude sickness. Most of them commonly use AP, Paracetamol for analgesic and antipyrexial purposes. It administers the determinental effects on function of clara cells by reducing the production of surfactant, bio-activation of various chemicals and carcinogenesis in the lung. Paracetamol is associated with hepato-nephrotoxicity with prolonged or high dose in human beings. The role played by clara cells in AP metabolism is a vital in respiratory system. The scientific study shows the high dose of AP, Paracetamol collapses the function of lung in human body.

Hence, the people and trekkers climbing at high attitude zones marked from 3,000 meters should not be commonly served with AP, Paracetamol.

5

Development Principle

Goal

The village tourism strategy has a long term perspective scenario with the goal to develop baselines so that the protected areas and villages (buffer zone) can minimise the cost of tourism and maximise its benefits. The basic aim of the strategy is to provide guidelines for village tourism development to the concerned authorities and the people in Chitwan.

Likewise, phase-wise development of village in Chitwan will be promoted with the local force and understanding.

Objectives

(a) To develop village tourism and its strategy by conserving bio-diversity while promoting park, village and village recreation.

(b) To enhance an ecologically friendly, community/village based tourism strategy and village tourism model through active villages and local User Groups' participation.

(c) To carry out an environmental audit of tourism activities on a regular basis.

Methodology

To achieve the above mentioned goals and objectives the following studies and surveys were conducted :

(*a*) Review of relevant literature on tourism and Royal Chitwan National Park.
(*b*) Use of secondary data.
(*c*) Discussion and observation.
(*d*) Key informant and group interviews/Participatory Rural Appraisal.
(*e*) Household baseline survey.
(*f*) Socio-economic and environmental conditions.
(*g*) Assessment of people's attitudes, User Group and Functional Group.
(*h*) Assessment of ecological impact and tourism carrying capacity.
(*i*) Hotels/lodges and village survey.

To calculate tourist's expenditure, purpose of visit, employment, use of cemented houses, gross income of lodges, tax revenue, tourist arrivals etc. interview methods with questionnaires were followed. The warden, officer, ranger, mobiliser, credit/community officer and related staff at Kasara and Sauraha were interviewed and records kept on a register were also taken for study. The local hoteliers/lodge owners, guides, naturalists, villages villagers, teachers, Hotel Association, Hotel and Community Development Committee, Branch Office of Taxation and other related persons were interviewed in Kasara (inside the National Park) and Sauraha, Bachhouli, Bhagara etc. (outside the National Park).

A few direct observations and Participatory Rural Appraisal (PRA) were also made. 102 tourists and 100 people were interviewed and participated in the discussions. The Department of Taxation in Kathmandu was also contacted for necessary data collection.

6

Village Tourism Strategy in Chitwan

BASIC INFRASTRUCTURE AND AMENITIES

Trails, Bridges and Frenches

Trails, bridges and trenches are commonly used in and around the National Park. They are supposed to be the basic infrastructure for park conservation and the village tourism plan in Chitwan.

The trail built from Sauraha to Kasara is not in good condition. Likewise, elephant routes and forest roads were also found to be in poor condition. Tourists will feel uncomfortable unless we develop the basic infrastructure. Practically, the trail is an important route for trekkers and local people. The wooden bridge made in Sauraha is not dependable. In the rainy season, floods spilled over the bridge and disrupted transportation. It also hampered the local economic business of life. Jeeps are required to run through the Rapti river at considerable risk.

Trenches were found not to be stone wall constructed in many places where this construction is necessary. Local people felt unsafe and they continually raised the issue of crop damage by rhinos.

Toilets, Drainage and Garbage Disposal

Toilets, drainage and garbage disposal are a regular part of daily life. The environment cannot be clean unless they are managed properly and systematically. Today, everyone is environmentally conscious. Nobody likes living in a dirty polluted environment. Basically, tourists like to see a pollution free society with fresh and cool air. Local villagers should solve their problems by promoting waste management plans. They need to build toilet and drainage facilities in their households so that health and sanitary conditions improve.

Improved Stove and Biogas Plant Technology

Improved stove and biogas plants are alternative methods of decreasing fuel-wood use in Chitwan. A family needs at least 10 kg. of fuel-wood per day. The Chitwan district contains a population of 3,54,488 people and 65,145 households (CBS, 1991).

They are mostly dependent on fuel-wood. The villagers living adjacent to the National Park should think of the importance of forest. Especially, they have to be environmentally conscious. The implementation of preventive measures relating to resource conservation is a must.

Improved stoves consume less fuel-wood and biogas plants give an option for an appropriate transfer of technology. Some of villages like Bhagha and Bachhouli have already started improved stove technology and biogas plants successfully.

Health and Sanitation

Health and sanitation is another basic primary need. We need sound health more than wealth. Sanitary measures, I feel, are goes ways of living. So let us not forget that prevention is better than cure. 'Health for all by 2000' is the holistic approach for mankind. It includes equitable distribution and a multi-sectorial approach... The 'People first' concept making health a public agenda is an empowering process for the people.

Travel in the jungle is a difficult task. Wild animals can hurt tourists and local people while walking in the forest. For this reason a health care service is necessary. A few health care services managed by Tiger Tops and KMTNC have already been established in villages like Jitpur and Bachhouli.

Villagers are very poor from the health and sanitation aspect. They still believe in the use of witch-doctors and traditional healers. Local people are backward in health care. A plan for the installation and management of rubbish bins and disposal containers in particular areas for waste management is required. Let us be very cautious that tourism is a fragile industry which is concerned with health and sanitation. Village tourism will not flourish until plans to eliminate environmental problems are in place.

Drinking Water and Village Communication Facilities

Drinking water and communication facilities assumed to be two separate mile-stones when considering infrastructure development. This two-pronged approach to government policies is proposed for improving the standard of public life. Every household needs drinking water and communication facilities, but these are constrained by the small income of household families.

Tourists search poor villages for a bottle of pure, cold water and can find none (Pradhanang, 1995). This state of affair affects tourism by indicating premature development. Drinking water is not only the basic need of the people, but is a universal need. Normally a local person needs 20 litres of water per day whereas a tourist consumes 2.5 times more.

Similarly, communication is equally important to inform and convince the people of the project's objectives. Today is the day when modern communications can pass the message around the world within a minute. One-way communication is useless and isolated. We need two-way communication by developing two terminals. Practically speaking, this refers to the different means of communication from one place to another. e.g. telephone, telegraph or television.

Safety and Security of Tourists

Tourists should experience a feeling of safety while travelling. The major priority is security of tourists for the host country and for the host family. One cannot lose one's life but rather be loved by one's self. Hence, security of tourism in the village must be a question addressed in the management plan.

Correlation with Other Sectors

The basic infrastructure is concerned with economic development. Construction of new trails, bridges, elephant routes and trenches assists the mobility of tourists and local people. They can easily go from one place to another. Similarly, the old trails, bridges and trenches should be restored to useable condition.

More importantly, toilet, drainage and garbage disposal are directly related to the public health. A clean environment directly leads to a green atmosphere. Basically, improved stove and bio-gas plant improve the living standards of local people on the one hand and reduce the consumption of fuel wood on the other. The whole process is a chain reaction and each is related with each other.

Opportunities and Potential

The provision of a infrastructure promotes village tourism alongwith the objective of bio-diversity conservation. The trails, elephant routes, bridges and trenches are prerequisites for development. Local people feel more safety when trenches are built on the boundary of their land. There is an immense potential for promoting village tourism in Chitwan. Many tourist related activities will appear in the country by creating a multiplier effect. The demand for various products such as poultry farming, livestock and handicrafts can boost the economy.

Constraints and issues

The constraints of infrastructure construction cost is very high when we talk of the building of bridges, forest fire-lines (trail), elephant routes, trenches and so on. The life of the poor people living in Chitwan is thus constrained. The talk of funding the construction of toilets, garbage disposal management and an efficient drainage system will be an enormous burden to the poor people when they have no food to eat. Their cash crops are constantly threatened by a lack of fencing with rhino proof trenches within the buffer zone.

For this purpose, the local people and government have no capacity to build up the basic infrastructure due to the lack of an adequate amount of investment. That is why tourism development is highly concentrated in the National Park alone and it has been unable to spread over to the villages of Chitwan.

MAJOR POLICIES AND STRATEGIES FOR DEVELOPMENT

Policies

1. To improve the existing forest trails, bridges, elephant routes, motorable forest roads and trenches throughout the important areas and build some new circular trails, bridges and trenches.

2. To conduct health and sanitation awareness programmes and establish Health Care services in Chitwan.

3. To build toilets and drainage and manage a garbage disposal system within the buffer zone.

4. To conduct a programme on improved stoves and bio-gas plants.

5. To prohibit the opening of new hotels in and around the National Park and to propose the removal of some of the existing hotels to new tourist sites.

6. To manage drinking water as well as communication facilities in villages.

7. To adopt security measures by managing community policy and establishing a network of sign posts. Travelling sites should be fixed within the jungle. No one should go to the forest haphazardly or alone.

Strategies

1. Trails and Bridges

The 19 km. long forest fire-line from Sauraha to Kasara should be restored to good condition. The existing elephant routes should be improved. The wooden bridges made in Sauraha should be expanded and the bridge in Jitpur should be well fenced. The trenches built in Jagatpur (especially wards No. 1 and 2) need to be improved by fencing and made rhino proof. The village roads of Bhagaha and Jitpur should be gravelled. A budget amount of NRs. 8,00,000 should be allocated by the Village Development Committee. Tiger Tops and Narayani Safari Camp, that frequently use the road, should help with this gravelling.

Proposed Bridges for Maintenance Directed to Sauraha Forest Road

The following bridges are in urgent need of maintenance :

1. Jarneli bridge (No. 1)
2. Dhukur Khola
3. Front of Jarneli
4. Back to Dhumriga
5. Charara Khola
6. Bahalpur Khola
7. Way to tented camp, Gaida Wildlife Camp

In addition there are 22 bridges (including small and big) on the road to Sauraha. They should be restored to good condition.

Proposed Bridges for Maintenance Directed to Kasara and Madi Forest Road

The following bridges are in urgent need of maintenance :

1. Ghatgaighat bridge
2. Bridge nearby Kasara
3. Around forest fire-line, Kasara
4. Around Gaur Machan and Chure Hill
5. Front of Dhurba check post (lying three bridges)

Necessity for Maintenance and Cleaning of Lakes

The following lakes require urgent attention to restore them to an attractive state :

1. Ghaila Lake (Ward No. 1, Jagatpur)
2. Kukur Lake (Jagatpur)
3. Devi Lake
4. Munda Lake (near Tiger Tops)
5. Tomor Lake
6. Lami Lake
7. Beesh-Hazara Lake.

Necessity for Building New Forest Roads

The following two-way forest roads should be built :

1. Sauraha-Daumre-Gaur Machan
2. Kasara-Tamor Lake-Chure Hill.

Necessity for building new bridges

The building of the following bridges is necessary :

1. Dhudhaura Khola nearby Rapti
2. Around Suki Var check post and Machan view Tower (three bridges)
3. Chitrasari Ghat around Budhi Rapti River.

Necessity for building new trails

The following new trails are required :

1. Around Raptighat (Area No. 1)
2. Around Raptighat and Dhudhaure river
3. From Sauraha to Gaida Wildlife Camp
4. Around Gaurighat (Especially southern side).

Necessity to Build New View-towers

The following view towers are proposed for urgent construction :

1. Around Jayamangala
2. From Sauraha to the southern forest
3. Around grassland.
4. Around Talmochan area No. 2
5. Velar Gadi

2. Health and sanitation

A health and sanitation awareness programme should be organised by the Parks and People Project with involvement and participation of the local people. Initially, the project should hire some sanitory experts to conduct grass root level workshop and seminars. A health awareness programme should be organised from time to time. In addition, the project should encourage the village Development Committee, NGOS, Hotel Association and local intellectuals to educate the local people.

3. Toilets, Drainage and Garbage

Toilets, drainage and garbage dumping areas should be built in every village community. Village should take interest by themselves. The Parks and People Project has to support the community based programmes. Sufficient amount should be allocated in the budget. Gradually, VDCs and NGOs should build public toilets, drainage and garbage disposal areas. For this purpose VDCs should allocate some of the budget in its annual programme. Also, NGOs can assist in the development.

4. Hotels and Lodges

The opening of new lodges in Sauraha should be prohibited and new tourist sites (villages) should be developed with joint cooperation of hoteliers, intellectuals and the National Park. Lodges should be graded by standard and maintain fixed prices. The discounted price system should be totally discouraged or abolished. Some of the local hoteliers must be encouraged to shift to new tourist sites away from Sauraha to maintain the balanced growth of tourism. The top priority should be given to the local people to develop village tourism in and around the National Park.

5. Stove and Bio-gas Plants

Prior to the resource conservation, the programme on improved stove and bio-gas plant should be massively implemented. The National Park should make a proposal to a relevant technical expert or the Agricultural Bank to launch the programme into real action. Some subsidies and loan facilities should be encouraged for the local people.

6. Drinking Water and Communication

The drinking water and communication facilities should be planned by local efforts. VDCs, NGOs and the National Park should support the programme. Especially, the VDCs should strongly lead by submitting a solid plan to the central government.

7. Security

The security of tourists should be guaranteed. Tourists coming to visit the National Park should be accompanied by a village guide and security guard. The emergency radio communication, or wireless, and first-aid health service provision should be managed. In order to provide a good standard of service, the National Park should charge a service fee. The provision of a mobile tea/coffee shop and a cold spot for refreshments could be facilitated so as to make jungle travelling more comfortable. For these purposes trained and skilled manpower should be developed.

VILLAGE TOURISM AND GROUP POVERTY ALLEVIATION

Based on the village tourism concept, several villages within the buffer zone can be promoted by programming various economic activities. The activities will deliver services to the rural poor for their upliftment. The households of the rural people can participate in economic development activities generally through group organisation processes thereby augmenting their overall welfare and income.

With the key philosophy of local development, efforts have to be made to generate economic activities at the grass root level through a village tourism approach. It supports the use of local resources *e.g.* land, labour, technology, etc. In order to promote economic activities, various tourism related occupation can be adopted as a model for an inter-linked development process. During the fiscal years 1975-76 to 1994-95 Asian development Bank/Nepal (ADB/N) has disbursed credit amounting to Rs. 2991 million of which Rs. 1767 million has been realised. The study report states that household income of small farmers in the rural area increased by 30%. Similarly, they improved in the use of farming methods (ADB Report, 1995).

Social and community development activities are the next important programme which can be taken, through the people participation approach, e.g. education, sanitation, drinking water, toilet construction etc.

Further, irrigation schemes, installation of power pumps, shallow tube-well and sprinkler irrigation, environmental conservation and women's development can be enhanced by their own efforts. Hence, Village Tourism Bank should be separately opened to facilitate the loans for village tourism development by which the rural economic development process can be started.

TABLE 6.1

Pattern of Internal Credit Facilities Investment in Meghauli VDC April-June 1997

Village tourism based activities	*No of beneficiaries*			*Very poor people benefited*	*Amount NRs.*
	Male	*Female*	*Total*		
Poultry	11	10	21	11	11,995
Vegetables	2	0	2	0	2250
Agriculture	27	17	44	19	23,116
Pig/goat/buff.	21	24	45	17	47,207
Shop	3	4	7	3	6,600
Consumption	18	7	25	10	17,867
Total	82	62	144	60	109,035

Source : Royal Chitwan National Park records, August 1997.

TABLE 6.2
Participation of User Groups in RCNP, December 1996

User Group	*Member*	*savings (NRs. mill).*
68	2,505	0.225

Source : RCNP records, December 1996.

Apart from this, poverty being a massive and complex problem, we can generate several economic activities through village tourism. Therefore, poverty can be eliminated by promoting groups of people living in the rural villages. Consequently, the real "rural trickle down" policy will be adopted by reducing the rural poverty of indigenous groups of people.

Village tourism is concerned with various village economic activities such as preparation of local food and beverage, indigenous accommodation facilities in traditional huts/houses, livestock, poultry farming. pig farming, cottage and small industries, agro-based industries, vegetable production, horticulture, dairy production, boating, fishing, bee farming, curio shopping, traditional culture shows etc. These are some of the village based products that can be professionally undertaken by the villages.

Tourism in Chitwan has been one sided tourism which has focused only on wildlife for the last 30 years. But, the taste and demands of tourists have changed. They want new products and attraction. These can be fulfilled by village based tourism and village activities. Village activities, which are very wide, should be identified from the viewpoint of the tourism market.

Correlation with Other Sectors

Village economic activities are intimately linked with village based tourism on the one hand, and they are concerned with agriculture, trade, industry and different occupations on the other. They are directly or indirectly related to village tourism. The village tourism plan aims to integrate the effectiveness of sound mobilisation to alleviate poverty development. Launched in the adjoining village of Royal Chitwan National Park (buffer zone), the User Group's participation has been found so effective that by the end of June 1997 a total of 68 organisations have been formed with 2505 members. For example, in respect of the internal credit facilities investment (ICFI) Rs. 1,09,035 was lent to 144 members in Meghauli VDC. Villagers utilised the credit facilities in different economic activities like poultry, vegetable, agriculture, pig, goat, buffalo farming, shop opening and consumption. It shows that more than 82% of villagers have been found to be directly or indirectly involved in tourism based economic activities. Table 6.1 & 6.2 indicate the pattern of internal credit and participation of User Groups.

Opportunities and Potential

Village tourism has been seen as a vehicle to drive through several economic activities. In this sense, we have immense opportunities and potential to develop local economy. Many more nature based and village based programmes can be undertaken as an extension of park recreation and buffer zone development. Basically, income and employment oriented business opportunities are coming to and fro.

So, the park serves the following potential goals :

1. Chitwan as a single tourist destination/First model park in Nepal.
2. Promotion to number one park in the world/Park tourism centre.
3. Enhancement of village tourism/wildlife tourism centre.
4. Plan as a revenue oriented park.
5. Generator of economic development for the rural people.
6. Marketing plan for the target group.
7. Creation of income, employment and government revenue.

Constraints and Issues

Tourism development in Chitwan is one sided and mainly concentrated in the National Park. It could not spread widely in the Chitwan district. The major constraint, I understand, is unbalanced growth of tourism. Similarly, the quality, high spending tourists being out of village reach are major issues for tourism area promotion.

Tourism in Chitwan is characterised by the complexity of the disparity between the high spending tourist and the low spending tourist. The inside tourism in the National Park is followed by quality, high spending tourists whereas the outside tourism, based in Sauraha, is predominantly patronised by low spending tourist.

Furthermore, the buffer zone possesses 37 Village Development Committees (VDCs) where several villages are still ignorant of the tourism development and its potentials.

MAJOR POLICIES AND STRATEGIES FOR DEVELOPMENT

Policies

1. To generate village economic activities by linking them with village tourism as much as possible.

2. To promote traditional communities as village tourism specialists.

Strategies

1. Village tourism, being a service oriented industry, is like a panacea for economic development. Tourism related activities should be spelled out for the mobilisation of local resources, skill and expertise.

The local people should be concerned with village development by employing various economic activities such as village guide, naturalist, tourism entrepreneurship, local handicraft development, travel and trekking skill development, traditional ornament manufacture, village based tourism development etc.

2. Rural traditional communities should be identified and

analytically brought into the programme. From the viewpoint of the tourism market, the old and ancestral objects must be preserved and revitalised as new products of tourism. The history of the ethnic group of people should be prepared along with their commodities such as old houses, stone taps, wells, temples etc. The village guide should explain the significance of the commodities by telling their history. For this purpose, a special village marketing plan must be developed.

MANAGEMENT OF VILLAGE TOURISM

Tourism is a goose that lays golden eggs. The golden eggs, I understand, are our reward earned from tourism promotion. Village tourism as a phenomenon, is concerned with river, sun, environment, rural society and household. It represents conservation, life style, experience, adventure and above all the nature and adventure oriented benefit to the local people.

The objectives of village tourism include helping tourists to plan a trip, choose a tour and minimise ecological impact. A village tourist should be considered as a responsible traveller. Village tourism guidelines are generally targeted at village tourists who generally would go to natural areas, parks and protected areas. Basically, a village tourism plan is focused on the target-group of tourists intending to participate in programme that provide local benefit.

Opening and Promotion of New Entry Point

Village tourism management plan needs some additional entry points to the National Park from the viewpoint of local people's benefit and to evenly distribute tourist flow. Some of the existing entry points ideally should be shifted or closed. Most of the villages are still out of the reach of the benefits of tourism. The pressure of tourists only concentrated in Sauraha. Tourist activities must be dispersed, mainly in villages. That is why elephant riding facility should be extended to Meghauli entry point and other areas.

Village Tourism Zoning

Tourism zoning system is an integral of the tourism plan.

Village tourism zoning regulations must ensure the preparation of sympathetic local land use plans for resorts, village and other types of tourism development areas. Reference must be made to zoning principles, zoning regulations and deliberate development standards like building style, density and height. Industrialisation is to be controlled near tourism development areas. It would not be compatible to tourism. Zoning helps maintain control of environmental pollution and degradation.

Regarding site planning, architectural and landscaping designs are determined with common practice. All proposed tourism development projects have to meet tourist standards as per the zoning regulations. Besides, tourist facilities and services are required to meet quality standards with regard to health, safety and sanitation. Regulations on licensing of hotels/lodges, restaurants, travel and trekking agencies and tour guides are necessary to operate.

In the villages of the buffer zone, tourism related retail shops like curio shops, souvenir shops etc. should be licensed by the Department of Tourism or the National Park.

Simultaneously, building regulations relating to site plans, carrying capacity plans and construction standards should also be considered with regard to tourist facilities.

'No regulation, no management' is the prime principle of tourism zoning in relation to a village tourism plan. In a developing area like Nepal, villages can be used as "village tourism zoning areas" for fishing, gathering, lodging sporting etc. The government should carefully implement zoning regulations in tourism sites.

Under the tourism zoning principles, the seven concessionaries and 53 lodges located in and around the National Park were found not to be controlled and categorised by any good system.

Tourism Information Technology

A village tourism management plan requires a tourism information technology. It relates with marketing, monitoring, demand and behavioral pattern of tourists. For an effective village tourism management system, information on marketing development and monitoring are very important. The information system can be better monitored if it is computer-based.

The system requires information about tourist arrivals, purpose of visit, nationality, accommodation (supply, type, location, occupancy rates), tourist expenditure pattern, attractions, facilities, visitation rates etc. In addition, information on tourist attitudes is required to be obtained from surveys and recorded information system.

The system can be used for monitoring and evaluating the programme implementation and effectiveness. The same data can be used for data analysis on marketing studies. It is the transfer of information technology system needed for a village tourism management plan.

Park Recreation

Park recreation has environmental, economic and social importance within the discipline of geography. Research on leisure, recreation and village tourism has not been grounded in a particular paradigm. There is a distinct relationship between the park recreation and the tourist who would like to enjoy experiencing the wild animals and nature in and around the National Park. The Royal Chitwan National Park has mainly two recreation facilities, namely nature-based and village-based programmes.

Basically, the park has wildlife recreation. Tourists can enjoy nature and bio-diversity. Naturalists claim that Nepal has 850 types of bird species. Out of them, Chitwan alone possesses about 500 bird species. In Nepal some bird species are found to be endangered and rare such as black shrike, spiny babbler and so on. Bird watching in the national park is a special attraction. Boating, fishing, swimming and camping are also favourite park-related activities. Canoeing with a visit to river side villages can be an attractive option for tourists. Additionally, floating houses and canoeing games can be new recreational items. Tourists dressing as professional fisherman, kumale, can enjoy traditional fishing techniques as a new experience. Tree planting by individuals whose names are given to "their" tree, e.g. Nancy tree, John tree, Ram Bhattachand tree Kawamura tree, Prince tree, Prime Minister tree, Millennium tree, Tourist tree, Love tree, Good luck tree etc. can be started to establish village tourist forest colonies in conjunction with the community forest for partnership programme.

Regarding park recreation facilities, there are two separate programmes set aside for inside tourism and outside tourism in and around the National Park. They are given below.

Inside the Park

Nature-Oriented programmes

1. Walk with tiger tracker
2. Day picnic
3. Boating
4. Kasara drive
5. Game drive (open Land Rover)
6. Nature walk
7. Walk with naturalist
8. Slide presentations
9. Watching flora and fauna
10. History of National Park lectures
11. Wildlife documentary movie
12. Jungle walk
13. Jeep safari
14. Bird watching
15. Elephant Safari
16. Camping site

Village Based Programme

1. Horse riding/pony riding
2. Coach drive
3. Village walk
4. Village tour by ox-cart
5. Nature walk (buffer zone)
6. Cock fight
7. Life style watching

8. Monkey show
9. Historical tour
10. Tamakhu with hukha enjoying
11. Swoyambar Watching
12. Kite flying
13. Village cultural tour
14. Village children watching
15. Small world experiencing

Outside the Park

Nature and village oriented programme

1. Elephant safari
2. Village walk
3. Ox-cart riding
4. Bicycle riding
5. Night walk
6. Bird watching
7. Camping
8. Swimming
9. Soft trekking
10. Monkey watching
11. Herb watching
12. Rhino watching
13. Tiger watching
14. Tree watching

All these programmes could not have been properly provided in lodge packages. Village activities are not sufficient for tourism recreation. They need to be further promoted with additional programmes. Village and village life can be enjoyed by tourism if we are able to manage village based tourism products. The possible programme can be identified as follows:

1. Village Life Watching

It can partially be managed as morning, afternoon, evening and whole day programme. The activities of farmers, shop-keepers and workers and thus, the life style of the village can be watched.

2. Farming Activities Watching

It is dedicated to different types of local occupation following sheep, crocodile and deer farming.

3. Rice Plantation Watching

During the season, rice plantation programmes are massively done as a seasonal activities in villages. More specifically, tourists can watch the traditional rice plantation method and style.

4. Worshipping and Village Religious Rites Watching

Chitwan is rich not only in the bio-diversity but in the cultural diversity as well. Bikram Baba in Kasara has great religious value celebrating a grand religious festival. Devotees from different places, including Indian religious tourists, pay homage to God. Similarly, Dev Ghat, Ayodhyapuri and Balmiki Ashram are also famous sites where village religious life can be spent for enlightenment (Nirvana—the way of salvation). Tourist guides can explain the religious significance to tourists by telling the story of Sita, hermit Basista, Panch Pandav and so on.

5. Local Games

Local games are also a recreational item. Sport events like Bagchal, Horse polo, Buddhichal, Kapardi, canoeing, race competition, swimming etc. can attract tourists as well as the host community. Well organised sporting events provide uniqueness and charm. Elephant polo organised sporting by Tiger Tops is an example in this respect.

Apart from this, we need local expertise as an asset for village tourism development. For this purpose training is a basic foundation for productivity. Every plan when confronted with any proposition requires training for implementation. Thus, training is essential for promoting village tourism.. Local people are encouraged to be involved in the basic tourism management training in housekeeping, lodge/hotel, cook, reception, travel and trekking guide.

Code of Conduct

A code of conduct is a watch dog followed by regulatory machinery for the strict operational function of the village tourism management plan. The plan seeks to develop a code of conduct covering the following aspects :

1. Park Office

The National Park needs a code of conduct to develop village tourism in and around the National Park. The park is a promoter of village tourism. Its role should be clear with an appropriate rule and regulation process.

2. Village Development Committee

The Village Development Committee (VDC), an arm of local government, is also responsible for developing village tourism. It is a safeguard for protecting conservationists, village tourists, villagers and hoteliers.

3. Tourists

Tourists are the customers who should know how to enjoy the National Park and surrounding villages. Their conduct should be guided by strict regulations framed to protect them, the park environment and the local inhabitants.

Tourist Code of Conduct

1. Love and pay respect to Nepal and local Nepali villagers.
2. Keep the environment sound by promoting Nepal style socio-culture life-style and village systems.
3. Do not try to change any religion and politics, sexual and social customs and manners.
4. Try to taste and obey the Nepali objects locally made.
5. Do not go by conflicting in any activity or issue.
6. Travel with permission from the concerned authority.
7. Consider and love Nepal and Nepali people as home and brotherhood.
8. Give and take something but understanding and sharing

TABLE 6.3

Projected Tourist Arrivals and Revenue from Tourism in and Around Royal Chitwan National Park

Fiscal Year	*1996-97*	*1997-98*	*1998-99*	*1999-2000*	*2000-01*	*2001-02*	*2002-03*	*2003-04*	*2004-05*	*2005-06*	*2006-07*	*2007-08*
Tourist arrivals	96,062	111,432	129,621	149,943	173,932	201,763	234,045	271,492	314,931	365,319	423,779	491,573
Revenue NRs. (million)	47.01	52.00	57.75	63.61	70.35	77.81	86.05	95.18	105.26	116.43	128.77	142.82

each other from your visitation.

9. Be always good and expect good from others.
10. Promote village tourism and visit the village of Nepal.
11. Do not try to involve in sexual affairs with anyone else.

(Pradhanang / KRC, 1996)

4. Village

The village is a store-house of nature and culture. Villagers should know their village tourism product by which they can earn a lot of money. They are the host families who should understand both the village tourist and the village tourism business.

In addition, the observance of the code of conduct should be incumbent upon supply agencies like hotel/lodges, tour operators, army offices and so on.

Correlation with Other Sector

The village tourism management plan is mainly concentrated in and around the National Park. That is to say, the plan is related to the people of the buffer zone. The plan aims at protecting both the conservation area and the buffer zone by minimising cost and maximising benefit to the target group of people. It has a chain relationship with tourists, park, villages, hotels/lodges, tour operators and local administration in their socio-economic activities.

Opportunities and Potential

We have very good opportunities and potential for a tourism economic growth model. Promoting village tourism in Chitwan means conserving the park and sharing the benefit with local people. Income and employment opportunities resulting from increased tourist activities definitely can be generated in the villages. Inside and outside tourism in Chitwan will, no doubt, also flourish.

The future potential of tourism development is encouraging and the projection of the tourist arrivals and tourism revenue has been estimated for 11 years (1997-98/2008-09) in and around the National Park. The estimation was done on the basis of four years' data as shown in Table 6.3.

Constraints and Issues

The main constraint is the lack of coordination and strong determination of the concerned authority in implementing the plan. Motivation of local people is another constraint for village tourism development. Prior to the resource conservation, tourism has not been given high priority. It has been a secondary activity relegated to a position of little importance. Today's issue, I feel, is the lack of an appropriate policy and plan for village tourism development.

MAJOR POLICIES AND STRATEGIES FOR DEVELOPMENT

Policies

1. To open new entry points to the National Park and manage wildlife species and local human behaviour in a more professional manner.
2. To determine the tourism zoning in Chitwan.
3. To establish a tourism information centre and arrange for transfer of information technology.
4. To spell out the park and village recreation activities.
5. To conduct training programmes relating to village tourism management activities.

Strategies

1. The Royal Chitwan National Park should open additional new entry points in the periphery of Kasara, Beesh-Hazare lake and Kumrose. Tourists should feel convenience and simultaneously local people should be benefitted with the opening of the new entry points.

2. The existing lodges/hotels inside and outside the National Park should be declared as village tourist lodges/ hotels of Royal Chitwan National Park. The lodges which are inside the park should be categorised as highest standard deluxe lodges for high spending tourists. Basically, inside tourism, if properly run, must be high revenue oriented to the nation. Similarly, the lodges which are outside the National Park should be managed by grading A, B, C, D, E & F as per the lodge criteria development system.

From the view point of tourist demand and local people's benefit, some essential entry point should be opened. For example, Beesh-Hazare lake should be developed using the three dimension principle.

3. The Royal Chitwan National Park should open a tourism information centre around the National Park in Ratnanagar or Tadi area, so that tourists can get information. The information centre should be well-equipped and facilitated with information technology, information services and documents.

4. The Royal Chitwan National Park should spell out the nature based and village based programmes as far as practicable. Tourists should enjoy different types of recreation, following park and village activities to the maximum extent. New programmes like tree planting by individuals (names) should be started by establishing village tourist colonies in conjunction with the community forest. Similarly recreation inside and outside of the park should be fully identified.

5. Training programmes relating to village tourism management activities should be conducted. The park authority, lodge owners and villagers should clearly understand how to please and influence tourist. Better accommodation, clean and hygienic food and a healthy environment should be managed by increasing knowledge and skilled manpower. For this purpose, training in food preparation, household management (house-keeper) etc. should be organised.

LOCAL APPROACH AND INSTITUTIONAL FRAMEWORK

The local people's approach and behaviour patterns deliver this village and institutional framework. The programmes will be fixed only when the people really feel the need for development. The people in the villages adjoining the national park are generally critical of wildlife. Their crops are frequently damaged by rhinos. The land gets no more options for better utilisation. The only choice is agriculture. Therefore, it remains unproductive. So, the local people should have tourism awareness as an alternative plan for their utilisation of land, labour and capital. They have to learn the significance of village tourism in promoting the buffer zone. Village tourism is a way for inter-linked development where various economic activities can be run by villagers themselves.

The Parks and People Project tried to build up the institutional framework by forming User Groups and Functional Groups in each VDC of the buffer zone. The User Group is a union of a large number of people from a specific place while the Functional Group is the combination of different User Groups from different areas. User Group as well as Functional Groups are, no doubt, the active labour by which every motivational action plan can be operated. The Parks and People Project can, if it is honest, play a vital role. Actually speaking the role of these groups will be positively undertaken in local people's participation.

The local institutional framework for village tourism development in the villages can be handled, with the participation of the local people, by conserving eco-systems and planning village tourism.

Village Tourism Awareness

Village tourism can awaken the human vision. It heightens awareness of one's own milieu. Travel to foreign lands enlightens a new perspective and critical appreciation in the method of viewing one's own community. Perceptions are often sharpened and the personal "data bank" enlarged. Travel represents human experiences following new knowledge, research and activity. Similarly, visitors are also influenced by the culture and lifestyle of the people observed in new visiting countries.

The relationship between people and nature is a must. As eco-system is composed of plants and animals. It is measured in terms of benefit-cost estimates of the value of species. Village tourism, in the Nepalese context, is closely associated with the park and village recreation activities. It is characterised by different names such as alternative tourism, appropriate tourism, ethical tourism, environment friendly travel, green tourism, soft tourism, sustainable tourism etc. Thus village tourism is primarily concerned with the direct enjoyment of some relatively undisturbed phenomenon of nature made and man made atmosphere.

Village Tourism Linkage

Village tourism is an industry which is affected by the law of economics. Village tourism, if appropriately developed, can create more tourism related business activities. Consequently, we can promote various forward linkage and backward linkage based industries such as livestock, vegetable, dairy products etc.

Additionally, a tourist visits a place and spends his money in that particular region. Part of this money become income for the people living in that region. Part of this income is spent which generates income for other to spend. A part of this income is again spent and so on. Thus, money changes hand a number of times and is spent and re-spent. The impact of this expenditure on the nation's economy will go on multiplying as it changes hands again and again. Thus, the greater the number of hands through which such money passes, the greater will be the beneficial effect on the Gross National Product and the National Accounts and *vice versa.* (Pradhanang, 1993)

Village tourism is a multi-dimensional phenomenon related to different sectors of the economy. These sectors are interdependent with coordinated effort. So tourist spending is new money entered into the village. It really assists with the improvement of local business in the area. The benefit of village tourist money goes to different people such as farmers, lodges, professionals, businessmen etc.

The conflict between the park and people emerged with the new concept of the buffer zone as a restricted area surrounding the National Park and wildlife reserves in order to provide facility for use and the regular supply of forest product to the local people. The government realised that conservation of the park is not possible without having local support and participation. With regard to park resource conservation, minimal human influence will only be possible when the local villagers get an option in fulfilling their needs.

UNESCO's Man and Biosphere Reserve Programme indicates core projected areas can be maintained by "buffers" which act as transition zones which filter human pressures from reaching the core area. A buffer zone may be defined as a projected area on which land use is partially restricted.

The act has made a new provision of revenue sharing ratio generated from the National Park. Out of the total revenue collected, thirty to fifty percent will be utilised for local community development. The User Group and the local villages will be empowered to enforce Buffer Zone Management Rules. The Buffer Zone development leads to a positive relationship between wildlife conservation and local people by minimising park-people conflict.

Department of National Parks and Wildlife Conservation (DNPWC) and Parks and People Project

To support the buffer zone, DNPWC has operated the Parks and People project, with the collaboration of the UNDP, since 1995. It has the objectives of improving the socio-economic condition of the people living in the adjoining VDCs while developing the buffer zone and enhanced local participation.

Besides, it has income generating community programme followed by community forestry development and tourism promotion in VDCs of Chitwan.

There are several villages in the buffer zone. They can be promoted by maintaining eco-system in Chitwan. The villages like Bhagaha, Meghauli, Jagatpur and Swargadwari can be promoted as village tourism is good for villagers. It will help the local people by increasing visitation of village tourists. Planners and community representatives can work more effectively together. In order to develop coordinated and socially acceptable tourism, a village management strategy is necessary. This is what we call sustainable tourism by promoting tourism destinations.

Local Government and Village Tourism

Local government should understand the planning of village tourism in villages. It should have a keen interest to promote village economy by conserving natural resources. Wild species are considered as eco-friendly animals. But, the anti-conservation monster is devouring our National Park. Our politicians, both national and local must play a more positive role in promoting and implementing sustainable tourism.

Local government via the VDCs, should form an effective tourism committee, consisting of various tourism related bodies such as User groups, Functional groups, intellectuals, representatives from different political parties and tourism experts.

Tourism Associated Organisations

There are several tourism associated organisations in Chitwan such as lodges/hotels, travel and trekking agencies, Hotel Association, culture centres and NGOs. Basically, they should concentrate more on developing village tourism in Chitwan. These organisations are directly related with tourists and the nation's culture. They ought to expand the village tourism business as well as preserve bio-diversity.

Loan Provision

Capital for investment is considered as the life blood for business and industry. The local people need investment capital and working capacity. The short term and long term loan provision should be facilitated by establishing village tourism bank to villagers to start the engine of economic growth. Thus, loan facility should be provided to Village Tourism Development Committee (Registered Social Organization) without collateral on the viability of the village tourism project.

Correlation with Other Sectors

People's attitude determine the prospect of planning. The concerned people lying on the row of active participation leads to the successful plan. Generally, User Group and Functional

Groups are two basic representative community mobilisers. They can torch light the perception viewing in the right direction. Village tourism is not a single individual business but is concerned with inter-sectional relationships. Several villages of the buffer zone are environmentally connected with conservation and village tourism management.

The tourism organisations (lodges,/hotels, travel and trekking agencies, Hotel Association, NGOs etc.) are generally concerned with the promotional activities of tourism. Additionally, these organisations are also related with the different segments of national and international tourism. The villagers are initiated to support village tourism. Schemes are necessary to prepare for the long-term development of village based tourism followed by balanced tourism. A large number of tourists are out of village reach due to lack of proper tourism management. Facts about the size of the tourism business should be widely stimulated in the nation. This will create a favourable atmosphere for area-wide tourism promotion in the country. The tourist organisations, local government and villagers must be actively functioning for an effective tourism development programme.

Opportunities and Potential

The success of village tourism development is mainly dependent on the support and coordianation of the various organisations associated with tourism activities. The villages of the buffer zone have a bright potential for village tourism development. The beautiful nature and bio-diversity call upon tourism to enjoy villages of Chitwan more. Tourists are generally interested in the way of life different countries they visit. So, tourism programmes can be extended to indigenous groups of people following indigenous attractions such as accommodation and architecture, traditional dishes and food, culture etc.

The village economy can be improved through village tourism planning by promoting various village products. Similarly, local employment can be generated through village lodge and village household management plans in villages.

Villages in the buffer zone are mostly accessible by road and aeroplane. Also, communication facilities are now improving.

Constraints and Issues

Village tourism is not a propaganda but a meaningful plan and proposition having a manufacturing nature. Mainly its organisational patterns independent on the business community and the calibre of programme and policy. A large number of people do not understand village tourism. They think it is a frivolous and superficial activity adding little to the economy. Consequently, they don't care to support village tourism programmes. These programmes have not been included in the long term development plans nor allocated in the budget estimation.

Village tourism is a complex phenomenon. Local government is responsible for searching an appropriate channel for perspective vision. The village tourism development programme in Nepal is still premature. Villages in Chitwan are found with an almost zero motivational attitude in the matter of village tourism. They are still unconcerned with village tourism in their ordinary business of life.

Some of the constraints and issues are listed below :

1. Village tourism programmes have not been supported either by top level national leaders nor by tourism business leaders.
2. Lack of understanding about the concept and importance of village tourism in Chitwan.
3. Absence of understanding and cooperation of business leaders in village tourism development.
4. Lack of priority in village based tourism development by local and national administrations.

MAJOR POLICIES AND STRATEGIES FOR INSTITUTIONAL FRAMEWORK DEVELOPMENT

Policies

1. To encourage local people through User Groups and Functional Groups in promoting village tourism in villages of the buffer zone.

2. To develop model tourism villages for tourism development in the buffer zone.

3. To conduct village based tourism programmes in Chitwan.

4. To create an open environment for tourist organisations and local people in building of institutional framework of village tourism.

5. To provide loan facilities to the villages for the development village tourism and the related activities.

Strategies

1. The Parks and People Project has already formed User Groups and Functional Groups in the buffer zone. They should be required to train and instruct, using village experts or professionals, in implementing village tourism plans. Similarly, they should be clear in providing inputs for village tourism development. In order to fulfil this task, a week long workshop/seminar on village tourism is to be organised by the planners. The concerned authority should subordinate to the User Groups and Functional Groups to activate the process of implementation. Further, village tourism programmes should be communicated through the Adult Literacy Campaign. Standard training material on village tourism development should be prepared for people's participation.

2. A few model tourism villages for tourist development in the buffer zone are suggested to intensify local people's understanding and build their confidence. These model villages represent the whole mechanism for tourism promotion in villages.

The following criteria are suggested :

1. Sites must be close to the traditional ethnic group of villages.
2. The village to be selected should be accessiable to road and aeroplane.
3. Villages should have a keen interest to develop village tourism.
4. Villagers should be united in the development of village tourism.

5. Atleast a minimum basic infrastructure should be facilitated (drinking water, roads, communications, health and security).
6. Village tourism marketing should be possible in promoting domestic and international tourism market.
7. Improved stove or bio-gas plants programmes should be undertaken.
8. At least, the village tourism professionals should be literate.
9. Villagers should form Village Tourism Development Committee.
10. A code of conduct should be developed with the mutual agreement of the villagers.
11. Village Development Committee (VDC) should be involved in, or support the tourism business.
12. Professional honesty and discipline should be maintained by all.
13. Under the village tourism regulations and discipline, there should be an opening for a village tourism partnership or joint venture with domestic (city/town hoteliers, travel and trekking agencies etc.) and foreign investors, if interested, in the villages. Similarly the village tourism development leadership should be basically handled by Nepali national.
14. The Habitat Plan of Action Strategies by supporting tourism village agents be considered.
15. The village women should be encouraged more in promoting village tourism.
16. The village tourism development regulatory and supervisory law should be clear-cut and simple.
17. The village should be famous for the specific product and adventure based activity.
18. Village tourism industry should be registered as per the village tourism act provision.

(Pradhanang, 1996)

For these reasons, Bachhouli village, Bhagaha village, Meghauli village, Swargadwari village and Jagatpur can be selected as model villages for village tourism. The planner of village tourism development should develop those villages as per the Parks and People Project programme schedule. In the initial phase, an adequate budget for village tourism should be allocated for promoting atleast two villages.

Regarding Tharu Villages, Tharu houses could be attractively made reeds plastered with a mixture of clay and cow dung as is Tharu's traditional practice. Mainly, the rectangular shaped and north-south oriented houses should be decorated with 'tika' patterns or with pictures of flowers, animals and plants. Also, roofs should be thatched or tiled. The tourist village model should be purely furnished by nature and local resources. The environment should be displayed through various traditional living picture such as a watch (view) tower, cultivated land, children playing on a traditional dehusker, pigeon's nests around the Tharu houses, women grinding lentils, Tharu art on walls, hats, head balance and fishing nets, hand made from forest products, and tattoo designs on a Tharu women's legs.

3. The User Groups and Functional Groups have already started different programmes such as vegetable production, adult literacy campaigns, livestock rearing, improved stoves, biogas plants, saving-credit programme etc. in the buffer zone. These activities focused as village based tourism directly or indirectly linked with village tourism (Table 6.1 & 6.2)

These groups should be supervised by the concerned authority from time to time so that they will remain as an active force in the villages.

Simultaneously, the field mobiliser of the Parks and People Project should understand his responsibility to motivate the directed programmes. He can be accompanied by additional staff familiar with village tourism if work load is heavy.

4. The environment for tourism promotion should be opened for welcoming tourist organizations and local people. The different travel and trekking agencies showing an interest to promote village tourism in villages should be facilitated with traditional houses and local delicious foods. Similarly, the local people must be well informed of the significance of

village tourism. The local villagers, with the help of the User Groups and Functional Groups, should build up the

TABLE 6.4

Tourist Arrivals in RNCP by Nationality for 1996.

Nationality	*Number of tourists*
USA	6,639
UK	6,101
Japan	4,173
Germany	4,034
Australia	3,186
Netherlands	2,862
Taiwan	2,462
Hong Kong	2,036
France	1,494
Switzerland	1,396
Italy	1,231
Belgium	1,124
Canada	1,504
Spain	886
Thailand	779
Israel	722
Russia	721
Sweden	709
Malaysia	587
New Zealand	535
Norway	474
Singapore	444
India	19,975
Nepal	27,808
Others	4,180
Total	96,062

Source : RNCP, Kasara

institutional framework of village tourism.

Basically, village tourism must stimulate the transformation of old and traditional houses and sites into completely new tourism facilities. It should bring new life and vitality while showing the traditional character and charm of villages in a professional manner. In addition, Botanical Gardens, Herb Centres and Indigenous Culture Centres should be developed as new park recreational attractions.

However, effective consultation with VDCs, local people, travel and trekking agencies, User Groups, Functional Groups, local tourism experts, professionals, political parties and intellectuals is recommended to build up the village tourism institutional framework.

5. The villagers should be provided with adequate loan facilities for enhancing village tourism promotion and its related business. In order to promote the model villages for village tourism, soft loans should be given to interested local villagers so that they can maintain their traditional houses within acceptable clean and attractive standards. Loans will be provided for the local villagers who are interested in following various village tourism activities.

Therefore, loans should be provided to villages like Bhagaha, Swargadwari, Meghauli, Jagatpur, Bachhouli etc. if they are requested. The saving-credit function should be more active and the Park and Peoples Project should also provide soft loans, not exceeding Rs. 1,00,000, according to the nature of the work plan.

Loan provision to poor villagers from the Development Bank, Agricultural Bank and Gramin Bank (Rural Bank) should be arranged by the concerned authorities.

MARKETING PROSPECT

Marketing of tourism for an area is very important. We talk of the prospective tourists. Tourists must be persuaded to visit tourist sites which they can enjoy. With regard to the integrated approach to planning village tourism in Chitwan, the plan must include a marketing aspect.

Market analysis, I understand, is a major portion related

to the area's attractions and economic development. For sustainable development, tourism marketing is a must. Carrying capacity analysis of the area is the next factor affecting the marketing plan.

Market and Tourism Product Relationship

A successful marketing programme is based on product and market. A tourism product is both what a host country wants to sell and what a visitor wants to buy. Village tourism needs a sound professional marketing approach for area promotion. For each projected area, the use of appropriate marketing and publicity methods are necessary such as brochures, direct mail, television, radio, newspaper, posters etc. Information on the National Park, highlighting checklists of flora and fauna and wild animals, must be distributed to the national and international markets.

Target Group

The target group of tourists coming in Chitwan is to be identified. The tourists who are lovers of nature and life style of people culture may be the target group of the park and village tourism market. The researchers, students, geographers, thesis writers, anthropologists, socialists, scientists, poets, novelists, films producers, naturalists, environmentalists, honeymooners, thinkers, peace lovers artists etc. of international universities, social institutions and abroad can be accommodated in tourism villages.

Nature and culture are great motivational factors of attraction to tourists. They are, for example, wild animals, fauna and flora, climatic conditions and traditional culture. In 1995/96 tourists arriving in the RNCP were recorded as 96,062 (including Indian and Nepali). The highest tourist arrivals in RNCP, by nationality, was USA (6639). UK (6101) and Japan (4173). The target group of tourist should be the USA, Western Europe and Asia. They love nature and culture as shown by the statistical data (Tables 4.1 and 6.4).

Marketing Action Plan

The marketing plan is related to the marketing objectives and strategy. The marketing objectives will be set by target following long, medium and short term periods.

Village based tourism promotes resource conservation as well as culture. The specific types of tourist market and potential tourist market segment services are managed by supporting standard services.

The application of marketing principles in village tourism is concentrated on a marketing mix on the basis of the user's behavioural profile, Marketing decisions are taken on the basis of tourist's behaviour, tastes, preferences and demand.

Basically, a satisfied tourist, is an ambassador of goodwill and friendship. He is the source of more tourism and brings friendship and relationship.

Domestic Tourism Market

The village based tourism is attractive to Nepali tourists. Nepali tourists intending to visit new areas would like pollution free sites. The National Park and its adjoining villages are appropriate sites for recreation either for domestic tourists or for international tourists. During 1995-96 the number of Nepali tourists that visited the Royal Chitwan National Park have reached 27,808. (Table 6.4).

Correlation with Other Sectors

The marketing tourism has good relationship with other sectors in the promotion of the national economy. It brings multi-faceted development in the transportation, accommodation and communication industries. The professional travel and trekking agencies revitalise tourism by adding new dimensions in the tourism business. It has, thus, a holistic approach to interlink development.

This new approach gives the signal for the development of the travel business as an industry. The travel and tour business has gained momentum since tourism is an effective industry. The travelling business is a creator of employment and income. A few tourist sites are initiated to identify with infrastructure facilities. For this, marketing is required to have prepared a more dynamic and innovative profile. A well publicised tourism product derives greater profit.

Opportunities and Potential

Tourism marketing creates widening of socio-economic opportunities. It sets up a new nation's social life, promotion of intra-regional and inter-regional understanding. Thus, a tourism marketing plan, I understand, is an effective way for social transformation.

The villages of Chitwan, will be promoted when they are qualified from the tourist point of view. Being a multi-segment industry, traditional houses, hotels, transporation services, tourist resorts, parks, recreation centre, sales of curios, handicrafts, jewellery etc. are created as potential business with good opportunities. Really, the attractive natural beauty of villages creates good potential for village tourism development.

Constraints and Issues

Marketing of village tourism in the buffer zone is a difficult task. It is not so easy to promote villages that a large number of illiterate people are living in. Their minds and thoughts are found to be very conservative and difficult to convince. They always talk about the crops damaged by rhinos even the text of the discussion is not relevant to the subject matter. Their brain and mind were brutalised by shock from the destruction caused by rhinos.

Similarly, building of infrastructure is the next difficult task in the village. That is why, marketing of tourism is not so easy as we talk. By and large, villages will be promoted. Tourism, I think, is an economic bonanza, but it is a multi-segment industry necessitating several infrastructure facilities such as roads, transport and communication services, hotels and lodges etc. These requirements need adequate capital. In developing countries like Nepal people suffering from poverty cannot invest such huge amounts.

POLICIES AND STRATEGIES FOR VILLAGE TOURISM MARKETING DEVELOPMENT

Policies

1. To prepare a marketing action plan for village tourism in the buffer zone.
2. To identify the target group of village marketing.

Strategies

(*a*) Marketing for village tourism in the buffer zone is a new strategy except for the case of Sauraha. There are 37 Village Development Committees (VDCs) in the buffer zone. A marketing strategy such as product market, distribution and pricing should be properly managed. In addition the promotional mix like personal selling, advertising and so forth points out the process of marketing strategies :

1. The ethnic groups of people living in the buffer zone be identified and their specialities should be perfectly known.
2. The cultural significance should be spelled out by ethnic group of people.
3. Villages should be selected by the prospect of tourist attraction.
4. Traditional houses of ethnic groups of people belonging to villages should be suitably monitored and decorated.
5. Villages should have resource conservation motive in Chitwan and Functional Groups.
6. The local community should have been involved in User Groups and Functional Groups.
7. All village attractions relating to sports, fairs, customs, bio-diversity etc. should be spelled out beforehand.
8. A special Village Tourism Development Committee should be formed by the initiation of User Group, Functional Group and Social Organization.
9. A list of households showing an interest in village tourism promotion should be prepared.

10. The minimum basic requirement should be fulfilled by all the Committees.
11. A code of conduct, discussed with local government, villagers, intellectuals, User Groups, Functional Groups and the National Park authority should be prepared as a village tourism promotion mandate.
12. Villages should be environmentally clean and healthy.
13. Village tourism promotional sites/villages should be supported by neighbouring villages. (Pradhanang, 1996)

(*b*) The target group of village tourism marketing should be high spending tourists who would like to experience the particular life style of Nepalese ethnic groups of people.

The tourists should be provided with traditional objects and traditional hygienic foods. A special menu of the foods of ethnic groups of people should be prepared so that tourists can understand the speciality of food values.

All objects being used in the village households should be nicely arranged and kept in an attractive old design. Initially, the average length of stay should be in the form of a 2 night 3 days package. The programme should be given alongwith the food menu in systematic order. Village tourism activities should be promoted as local specialists. Ghungi (local snail) a delicacy of the Tharu people can be a part of a delicious cuisine to tourists Beach tourisms could be introduced to the surroundings of the Reu river in Ratnegau of Madi. So beach tourism has to be developed as a new village tourism product.

Village Tourism Development Committee should consult with the seven concessionary lodges for the promotional marketing of village tourism. Village religious tourism in Bikram Baba site, Ayodhyapuri (Dropadinagar) of Madi and Balmiki Ashram should be developed for religious tourists especially those of Indian and Nepalese origin.

In Madi, bridges across the Reu and Rapti rivers should be built soon. The budget allocated for bridge construction by His Majesty's Government should be implemented promptly.

The Royal Chitwan National Park should be extended. Beesh-Hazare lake should be promoted as a new village tourism product having attractions like canoeing and the establishment of a bird watching centre. It should be developed by the three dimension principle i.e. village community forests, village tourism promotion in the adjoining villages and the extension of the park. Some of the villages lying in the buffer zone can be promoted like Ganganagar, Devnagar, Salleni, Simgadhi from the stand point of tourism. The new entrance gate and tourist information centre should be opened here. There are some other villages namely Katsikari, Gauriganga, Kasharbagh and Semalgairi around the lake.

Canoeing should be improved by extending new village programmes. For instance, village walks and birds watching programmes at the river side can be included. Villages like Badreni and Malpur should be promoted as centres for village life and bird life. A story of bird life and a story of village life can be sketched by the living pictures of villagers and birds. Birds watching in different styles should be presented by explaining birds. Birds' nature and life style, chirping, breeding, flying, plying are interesting to watch. Bird call (language) is interesting to study for human beings. One such, the baya weaver, is a good example of species who compete for a mate by using their nest building skills demonstrating the challenge for the male bird to attract the female bird. Migratory birds like ruby shelduck and storks can be watched. Bird watching can be a special programme for a weeklong stay by tourists. Birds watching programmes can be developed at the following tourists sites :

1. Hatisar, Sauraha-southern Dhumre Khola-western Raptighat-back to the visitor centre, Sauraha.
2. Jayamangala-ghat, Simaraghol, Padampur VDC for marsh land bird watching.
3. Dudhaura site in area No. 3 of riverine forest.

Forty to one hundred and fiftytwo bird species can be watched a day in these spots. Some of the popular species are pied wagtail, scarlet-breasted sunbird, lora, paradise fly-catcher, Indian roller, Blue-bearded bee-eater, crested serpent eagle, moustached parakeet, intermediate egret, little egret and so on.

The Tamang ethnic culture, living style, dancing, singing and their life history should be displayed as part of the village programme for tourists. A story of the Tamang ethnic group should be prepared as a new tourist village product highlighting the unique behaviour and life style of the Tamang community, Basically, anthropologists, sociologists and researchers will be attracted to these programmes.

Programme on vegetation watching should be set out :

1. A programme on grassland in and around the National Park.
2. A programme on sal forest located at 500 metres above the sea level.
3. A programme on riverine forest successively processing from 'Kasha-Susoo-Khar and silk cotton' can be given to botanists even for a month. As an illustration, grassland and riverine forest in Bhelarghadi and sal forest in Nandatal are suitable places.

New trekking programmes with village spots in Chitwan should be set up as follows :

Tentative 12 day trekking programme

1. Sauraha-Ghatgai (1 day)
2. Ghatgai-Ghatgai check post-Tamor-lake-Southern Dhurbaghat-Bankatta check post-Dhurbaghat (1 day)
3. Dhurbaghat-Sukibhar view Tower-Bhimse check post-Meghauli (1 day)
4. Meghauli-Tiger Tops-Devi lake-Narayani river crossing-Navalpur (1 day)
5. Navalpur-south Tushakhola-Landaghat-Nawalparasi (1 day)
6. Nawalparasi-Temple Tiger-Tiger Tops-Bhimle check post-Meghauli (1 day)
7. Meghauli-Bimle Check post-Sukivar-Bankatta Check post-Gopal check post-Madi (Bankatta residents) (1 day)
8. Bankatta Basti-Bhote Simra-Kalyanpur, Madi (1 day)
9. Kalyanpur-Reu river-Ayodhyapuri VDC, Madi (1 day)

10. Ayodhyapuri-Babai check post-Amuwa check post-Thori village (1 day).
11. Thori village Amuwa check post-Chure hill-Bhimpur checkpost, Padampur (1 day)
12. Bhimpur check post-Gaida Wildlife Camp, tented camp-Dudhauraghat (Bridge No. 3)-Sauraha (1 day).

Programmes with Village

1. Sun rise watching from Jayamangalaghat-Padampur and Ghatgai
2. Sun set watching from Raptighat, Sauraha.

Fishing Village

Fishing village can be watched at the banks of the Narayani River. The Bhote and Kumale are the ethnic groups of people whose traditional professions are fishing. The programme for fishing village should be set for tourists to show them and experience how the local villagers catch fish. The moment tourists become a fisherman by wearing the traditional dress, a dramatic sequence of the fisherman's play will be exposed. Tourists can enjoy fishing by accompanying local fishing experts. For preparation local people should be provided loans or aid should be provided to them.

Wild Plant Dishes

Tourists can be served with local wild plant dishes for a new taste and experience such as Sisnu (nettles), Chaiu (mushrooms), nigro, sipligan, late. Similarly a wild plant named "Ashare pat" is very useful plant which is mostly preferred by Indian tourists. It makes lentils tasty when mixed with boiled ghee. Wild fruits like Bayar and Kusum are tasty. Local people should be introduced to marketing possibilities.

Seasonal Attractions

1. During December "tori flowering" is interesting to watch.
2. During October and November grassland watching is interesting.

3. During winter seasons (January to February) silk cotton flowering is interesting to see.
4. At the end of the spring season the silk cotton is interesting.

Tourists are interested in camping in the jungle. Campsite should be provided with necessary goods and services. At least 25 tents should be managed.

Stick Dance Centre in Village

A silk dance centre should be developed at Tharu villages like Simchhai, Campatol, Bhandara, Dorangi and Bachhouli thereby promoting Tharu people and culture. Village culture should be developed professionally. It is certain that tourists would like the unique culture of the villages followed by typical folk dance and song of the ethnic groups of people.

Local Handicraft Promotion

Local handicrafts produced in the villages should be promoted by highlighting local specialities through tourism marketing. Items such as Khurpi Thyak (a special type of knife and case), Ganja Katne Katari (a cutting vessel), chulesi (a special type knife), Kachiya (a local crooked knife), Kartal (musical instrument made of wood), Katbas (stick made of special bamboo) and Tharu ornaments having 32 different varieties made of silver and gold. For the promotion of these products, small loans should be granted to the local professionals.

Market Promotion by Competition Law

The market should be promoted by perfect competition. Tourists, I understand, are highly conscious customers or consumers who have the right to make the choice of their preference. Regarding liberalisation in the competitive market, competition law should be maintained.

Village Marketing by Purpose

Village Tourism marketing should be imposed by the purpose of tourists. There are tourists visited by different purposes such as wildlife (35%), human behaviour (4%), wildlife cum human behaviour (55%) and other (6%). (Table 4.1). Age determines the nature of business and demand for goods and services. The majority of age factor (26-40 years age group) shows that tourists coming to Chitwan are young . They should be provided that recreation facilities like honeymoon, spending holiday, playing cards, talking, relaxation, dancing, picinicing, nature sightseeing, moonlight watching, opon recreation hall. Above all, the village based tourism activity should be promoted.

Religious Village: Nepalase Haridwar

Dev Ghat has been popular day by day from the viewpoint of village religious tourism. It is next to Haridwar. The Hindu people from the kingdom of Nepal, especially from Kathmandu, and India would like to spend their retirement life in devotion of God so as to get peace and prosperity. As a matter of fact, people's ultimate goal has been to get Nirvana (way of salvation). About 600 persons from Kathmandu, 150 persons from Biratnagar and others purchased land for their settlement for peace and old age purpose. (Interview/study) Hence the religious village based tourism should be flourished by extending the vision of Nepalese Haridwar as per the demand of the domestic as well as Indian tourists, necessary arrangements should be made by the concerned authority and government.

Tourism in Chitwan

Inside tourism in the national park is purely a commercial tourism supported by different recreation facilities and luxury. Ecologically speaking, inside tourism is sophisticated. But, simultaneously, "If he pays, it stays" is the principal of sustainability for a resource conservation and village tourism management plan. It should be highly revenue oriented tourism for the nation. The target group of tourists should be high spending tourists. High spending tourists are allowed for high expenditure. Village based activities for the promotion of village tourism should be expanded. Mass tourism should be totally discouraged. A "protect-use-benefit" principle should be applied to the modality of bio-diversity conservation and village tourism. Inside lodges should have good relationship with the villagers. Poultry, farmed by Tiger Tops, should be voluntarily handed over to local people on lease. A monitoring unit should be developed for village tourism management and control.

Outside tourism in also equally important. The budget tourist and medium class tourist should be the target group of outside tourism. Several villages lying in the buffer zone should be promoted on the basis of planned tourism. Tourists would like to watch human behaviour of villagers alongwith the wildlife species. Economically speaking, outside lodges should be revenue oriented to the nation.

"Give and Take" Programme

Tourists care to travel for getting something and the host country or host communities also want something. "Something for something and something for anything" is the human nature for getting. The environment, thus, should be forum for tourists and the hosts people who can exchange views, culture and knowledge. Consequently, this "give and take" environment creates a school of thought in village tourism.

Finally, we should follow the human to human relationships of tourism, the human to God relationship of the culture and religion and the human to nature relationship of nature.

7

Environment

Environmental Audit

Man progress, nature loses—this has been the story of the man and the environment. Environmental and ecological degradation is caused by man's activities when a massive project is undertaken.

The word is losing about 7.5 million hectares of closed forests and 3.8 million hectares of open woodlands in the tropics each year and one million hectares is disappearing in India each year. Besides, it was estimated that over 15 percent of the tropical forest will be lost by the year 2000 in India. Similarly, Nepal is faced with ecological problems with resulting heavy losses. But the national study has not taken this into account at all. Tourism development may destroy the natural eco-system such as air pollution, destruction of forest, river pollution, traffic congestion and so on. Ecological impact has certainly been taken so far as the tourism development in the Royal Chitwan National Park is concerned. During tourist season at least 20 vehicles daily run inside the National Park where secondhand jeeps produce carbon monoxides emissions, sulphur and noise pollution. The noise can be heard even from a 2 km. distance. Burning grassland creates serious ecological impact especially to the aquatic animals. Several insects, trees and plants were killed. It is estimated that more than thousand insects and plants were eliminated.

A large number of elephants (68) are living in the National Park. They spoil silk cotton trees by breaking and eating them. Again birds living on the tree died. Several plants are damaged by elephant walking. Generally, an elephant damages at least 4 sq. ft. forest plant with its every step off trail in the jungle.

Wild animals lost their natural fright by increasing adaptability due to the frequent visitations and noise made by tourists in the forest environment. Tigers in RNCP gradually became mediator and attracted to domestic animals.

Lodges inside the National Park have been spread over 12 sq. km. That is why, tourism affected the eco-system for wild animals free movement. For example, a wild elephant requires at least 20 sq. km. land for its free movement. Lodges disturbed their movement when there are crowds of tourists and tourism related people inside the National Park. Similarly, a rhino requires at least 4 to 7 sq. km. area for its movement. A tiger (male) that needs 35-45 sq. km. area could run 60 km. within 24 hours (Interview : Naturalist inside lodge).

The study report states that 15,912 kg. of fodder from the park is used every day to sustain 78 elephants. An elephant needs an average 250 kg. of fodder a day (Information, RNCP)

The park also has to meet the fuel-wood needs of 312 persons as each elephant has a three person crew. A family in the village used an average of 10 kg of fuel-wood per day.

Tigers killed by poaching during 1991-1996 was recorded at 16 (Table 3.13). It is a terrible destruction if eco-system deteriorated by anti-nationalists. Construction of lodge/hotels in Sauraha has destroyed the land's ecology. The eco-system was automatically damaged when lodges were built, by lemon grass dominated grassland and result was that the grass was not preferred to eat by deer, rhino and elephant.

There are used batteries thrown away by tourists and tour operators in the jungle. It affected the eco-system seriously. The carbon spread in the jungle turns into poison. Several plants and insects were found to be affected. Fuel-wood consumed by lodges inside the National Park was estimated at 500 cubic feet per day in the tourist season. (Interview : guides) Garbage thrown inside the jungle created pollution.

Furthermore, outside lodges also threw away garbage, plastic bags and empty bottles at the roadside. It showed the environmental pollution.

There are 1600 local people employed inside the lodge and 444 people employed outside the lodges in and around the National Park. A total of 96,062 tourists visited the National park (RNCP/Kasara 1997). These people created pressure and deteriorated the environment. More than 300 wood cutters are undesirably engaged inside the lodges. (Interview/observation)

MAJOR POLICIES AND STRATEGIES FOR ENVIRONMENT CONTROL

Policies

1. To operate the method of minimising ecological degradation from tourism in and around the National Park.
2. To assess the ecological impact from the village tourism development every two years.

Strategies

1. Every lodge owner or hotelier should adopt the "keep the environment clean" camping. No one, should be allowed to pollute their surroundings as a result of tourism activities. A specific garbage dumping area should be fixed so that dustbins can easily be dropped in a particular place.

Secondhand vehicles in poor condition should be disallowed to drive in and around the National Park. In addition, a new mini bus service should be introduced. Every vehicle entering the National Park should be checked beforehand. Measurement of emission is a must. A carbon tax would be a relatively effective measure for reducing carbon dioxide emissions. Basically a command and control regulatory system in the form of a green tax or village tax as well as a "polluter pays" principle should be applied to fulfil the pollution control target.

2. The National Park authority should audit the environment pointing out tourism in Chitwan every two years.

Ecologists, environmental auditors and environmentalists should critically examine and evaluate the ecological and environmental degradation affected by the tourism business.

The physical, social, economic, biological and psychological impacts should be assessed. That is to say, carrying capacity should be calculated as for the season, time, facility, design, environment, demand of tourist etc. Guidelines for village tourists should be developed with disciplinary regulations and order that "Pack out what is packed in". Ecological guidelines should be prepared with the principle of preserving and managing principle of the eco-system like garbage disposal systems, human waste treatment, firewood collection, campfire and campsite placement, trails, driving or boating behaviour, endangered species protection, looking distance for wildlife viewing, and photography, touching animals, control of noise levels (radios, cameras, vehicles), protection of clean water supply, purchase and collection of natural souvenirs etc.

3. The air of Chitwan is seemed to be foggy due to increase of vehicles and factory emissions before rainy season. The way to get rid of sulphur in the emission all of the chemical fertilisers are produced from sulphur. Sulphur can be utilised to improve soil in Chitwan. It is better to produce from emissions rather than import fertilisers from foreign countries. Japan in this sector, can provide technical cooperation.

8

Evaluation

Monitoring and Evaluation

The principles of monitoring and evaluation can be applied to all kinds of plans. They can be operated to every aspect of planning strategy. Monitoring is necessary for village tourism development plan and programme, project development and village tourism marketing. It provides sensitivity for developing programmes.

Actually, monitoring is used to evaluate the overall village tourism management policy, plan and programme for achieving the objectives of the project. Some experimentation is required to justify the appropriateness of project implementation.

Monitoring should be taken on the formal and structural basis regarding economic, environmental and socio-cultural analysis. Tourist's attitudes about their experiences in the tourist site should also be known. Evaluation is also equally important to take corrective measures alongwith the monitoring system of tourism promotion. Monitoring and evaluation tasks to be conducted are suggested to carry out the project smoothly. The following tasks are required for monitoring and evaluation :

1. To monitor and evaluate the project areas implemented by the park authority as per the suggested objectives and goal.

2. To assess the social, economic and ecological impact of village tourism development in and around the National Park. Also to examine the park's carrying capacity of tourists, local resources and infrastructure.
3. To monitor village tourism development systems in the buffer zone.

9

Conclusion

Conclusions and Recommendations

The specified issues, potential and analysis show that we need special effort and attention paid to the implementation of a village tourism strategy and its plan. It is, on the one hand, a labour intensive industry and, on the other, a capital intensive process. Tourism is a meaningful proposition and now is the time to workout an appropriate strategy for its planned development.

Planning for tourism is an integral part of the overall national plan for economic development. Specifically, village tourism in Chitwan is highway to overall tourism development. The success of tourism implementation and development is largely concerned with the principle of "the right plan, at the right time, in the right place, by the right person." It will be the formula for achieving "the national tourists asset." Tourism planning suggests an integrated development of tourism resource and tourist activities to derive the optimum benefits to the people and to the country and to provide satisfaction to the tourists.

In order to achieve the desired goals and objectives immediately, short term, long term and perspective tourism related projects should be implemented. A different territorial level of plans, such as micro and macro, should be taken into consideration.

In order to develop village tourism a few major concluding notes are recommended below :

1. Village tourism should be extended to other parks and adjoining villages (buffer zone). Areas to consider, include Bardia National Park, Makalu-Barun National park, Langtang National Park, Rara National Park, Khaptad National Park, Koshi Tappu Wildlife Reserve, and so on.

2. Tourism from the grass root level or tourism involving the people as in, for example, village tourism, must be started for the balanced growth of tourism in Nepal. This is the starter for the tube-light that will eliminate the darkness of our current school of tourism economic thought.

"There is no easier means of economic development than village tourism for this generation in my country, Nepal. Until we start interlinked development in this country, which is known as a country of villages and make these villages saleable on the international tourism market, the economy and well being of the people and the nation cannot progress." (Pradhanang, 1996)

3. Prior to the resource conservation policy, priority should be laid down as per the importance of both tourism and conservation. The DNPWC and the Ministry of Forest and Conservation should set a clear and distinct policy by giving the priority to conservation first and tourism second. Tourism is, thus, like a panacea for economic development followed by local people's benefit to achieve the desired objectives of preserving the nation's cultural and natural heritage while ensuring the upliftment of the indigenous population.

4. The existing 7 concessionary lodges should not be narrowed down the monopolistic atmosphere. Instead, they should take serious concern with common people and welfare through the development of village tourism in Chitwan. The local villages and villagers ought to be economically benefited by tourism industry. Thus the equitable income distribution policy should be tactfully scheduled for the welfare of all the tourism entrepreneurs and local people.

5. The village tourism concept should be followed as the

'mantra' or appropriate guideline as well as the basic infrastructure development menu for national tourism development.

Finally, the lodges of Chitwan should be further promoted with a high economic growth rate of return on the one hand, the village tourism should be accommodated in the grass root with necessary infrastructures and understanding on the other side.

Bibliography

Aderhold, Peter. *The European Holiday Market for Developing Countries 1995.* Copenhagen : Institute for Tourism Research plus Planning August, 1995.

Atlanta 2000, institute of Ecology. The University of Georgia. *The Ecologist* (August/September 1977). UK : Ecosystems Ltd. 1997.

Amatya, Birendra Man, *The Clara Cell as a Target of a Cetaminophen (AP, Paracetamol)* Resident of Surgical Pathology, Tokyo Medical & Dental University/Kathmandu Research Centre, Tokyo, Japan, 2001.

Banskota, Kamal and Upadhyay, Murari. *The Makalu-Barun National Park and Conservation Area Tourism Management Component.* Kathmandu : Department of National Parks & Wildlife Conservation, HMG/Nepal, November 1990.

Barnard, Bruce, *"Does Business Want a Green Europe ?"* Europe p. 22. April 4, 1996.

Bolton, Melvin. *Royal Chitwan National Park Management Plan (1975-1979),* Kathmandu : UNDP/FAO Project Working Document No. 2, 1975.

Central Bureau of Statistics, *Population of Nepal (Population Census 1991)* Kathmandu : HMG/Nepal, National Planning Commission Secretariat, 1994.

Cogswell, Robert, *"Doing Right by the Local Folks : Grassroots Issue in Cultural Tourism",* Tennessee Business 6:3-16 No. 1,1995.

CREST, *Tourism for Mountain Community Development Case Study Report on The Annapurna and Gorkha Regions of Nepal,* Kathmandu : ICIMOD, 1995.

Doebele, Justin. Boutique Resorts, Forbes Global, March 6, 2000.

Department of National Parks and Wildlife Conservation, *Regional Symposium on the Conservation of the Royal Bengal Tiger*, Kathmandu : WWF Nepal program, 1998.

Department of National Parks and Wildlife Conservation, *Annual Report 1998/99* (Shrawan 2055-Asadh 2056), Kathmandu : DNPWC, 1999.

Department of National Parks and Wildlife Conservation, *Wildlife Nepal, Newsletter*, March-April, 2000.

Forbes Global, May 6, 2000.

Garratt, K.J. *Sagarmatha National Parks, Management Plan,*

Kathmandu : HMG of Nepal/New Zealand Cooperation Project, 1981.

Geis, Don and Tammy Kutzmark. *"Developing Sustainable Communities :*

"The Future is Now" Public Management 77: 4-13 August, 1995.

Gurung, K.K. *Heart of Jungle*. London : Andro Deutsch Limited, First Edition, 1983.

Gittinger, J. Price. *Economic Analysis of Agricultural Projects*. Baltimore and Sons London : The Johns Hopkins University Press, 1974.

Gen Oceania, *Global Eco-village Network Newsletter*, Volume 1, Issue 3, December 1996.

Gurung Dibya, *Tourism and Gender, Impact and Implications of Tourism on Nepalese Women*. Kathmandu : ICIMOD, 1995

HMG of Nepal, Department of tourism, *Nepal Tourism Master Plan*, Kathmandu : HMG of Nepal, Department of Tourism December 1972.

HMG of Nepal, Ministry of Finance, *Budget Speech of The fiscal Year 1997-98*, Kathmandu : HMG of Nepal, Ministry of Finance, 1997.

HMG of Nepal, Ministry of Finance, *Economic Survey fiscal Year 1998-99*, Kathmandu : HMG of Nepal, Ministry of Finance, 1999.

HMG of Nepal, Department of Tourism, *Annual Statistical Report 1995*.

HMG of Nepal, Department of Tourism, *Annual Statistical Report 1998*.

IUCN-Nepal. 1999.

Kandel, Prem Narayan, *People's Participation in Park, Management : A Case Study from Royal Bardia National Park*, Kathmandu : WWF, April 1994.

Kathmandu Research Centre, *Uncollected Costs Rs. 547,946 Daily,* The Rising Nepal, September 23, 1994.

Kathmandu Research Centre, *Nepalese Tourism Loses Rs. 227 M Due to Plague,* The Rising Nepal, February 15, 1995.

Kathmandu Research Centre, *KRC Emphasizes Village Tourism,* The Rising Nepal, April 20, 1995.

Kathmandu Research Centre, *People to Suffer Loss Due to Water Shortage,* The Rising Nepal May 28, 1995.

Kathmandu Research Centre, *Mane Gaun : Model for Village Tourism,* The Explore Nepal, December 28, 1995.

Kathmandu Research Centre, *Dumping Tourism in Nepal,* The Samacharpatra, February 14, 1998.

Kathmandu Research Centre, *Paryatanko Nepal Basne Abadhi Badhdo,* The Gorkhapatra, January 16, 1996.

KMTNC, *Royal Chitwan National Park : An Assessment of Values, Threats and Opportunities,* Kathmandu : KMTNC, October, 1996.

KMTNC, *Conservation for Development, Annual Report, 1996.* Kathmandu : KMTNC, 1997.

KMTNC, *Buffer Zone Policy Analysis of the Royal Chitwan National Park,* Technical Report, 1998, Kathmandu : KMTNC, 1998.

KMTNC, *Prakriti, Volume 1, No.* 2, Kathmandu : KMTNC, March, 1997.

Lindberg, T. Chandra. *Wild is Beautiful,* Kathmandu : S. Devi, Lalitpur Colony, 1981-82.

Milton, John P. and Binney, George *A. Ecological Planning in the Nepalese Terai, USA* : WWF and The Sierra Club Foundation, August 1980.

National Planning Commission, HMG of Nepal, *Approach To The Eighth Plan (1992-97)* Kathmandu : NPC, HMG of Nepal, April 1992.

National Planning Commission, HMG of Nepal. *Vikas Vol. 16, No.1* Kathmandu : NPC Secretariat, Nepal, June 1996.

National Planning Commission, HMG of Nepal. *Approach To The Ninth Plan,* Kathmandu : NPC, HMG of Nepal, August 1997.

Nepali, Rohit Kumar at. *The Makalu-Barun National Park and Conservation Area. Community Resource Management Component.* Kathmandu : DNPWC/HMG of Nepal and Woodlands Mountain Institute. November, 1990.

Nepal Human Development Report, Kathmandu : Nepal South Asia Centre, 1998.

Parks and People Project, *Annual Progress Report 1996,* Kathmandu : PPP, 1996.

Pradhanang, Surendra Bhakta, *Tourist Consumption Pattern and Its Economic Impact in Nepal.* Delhi : Adroit Publishers, First Edition, 2000.

Pradhamang, Surendra Bhakta, *Eco-tourism in Chitwan,* Seminar Paper, Kathmandu, Nepal, 1997.

Pradhanang, Surendra Bhakta, *Faith and Nepal's Village Tourism Development Concept,* the Working paper presented in Matsumotto City, Japan, July, 2001.

Pradhanang, Surendra Bhakta, Village Tourism: *A New Concept in the History of Nepal's Tourism Industry,* Business Age, March 1999.

Pradhanang, Surendra Bhakta, *"A Review of Hotel Industry, with Special Reference to Capacity Utilisation of Hotels of Kathmandu."* Tribhuvan University, Kirtipur, 1978.

Pradhanang, Surendra Bhakta, *"Nepami Bhoya : A Traditional Scientific Nepali Balanced Feast" Proceedings of National Conference on Science and Technology,* Kathmandu : RONAST, April 1998, P601.

Pradhanang, Surendra Bhakta, *Gau Paryatan Ra Gau Darshan, Abadharana Patra,* The Sagarmatha, March 19,1997.

Pradhanang, Surendra Bhakta, *Gramin Paryatanko Abadharanale Paryata Udhyogma Naya Ayam,* The Kantipur, November 1995

Pradhanang, Surendra Bhakta, *"Scientific Tourism - A Test in Nepal" Proceedings of National Conference on Science and Technology,* Kathmandu, RONAST, 1993.

Pradhanang, Surendra Bhakta, *Gang Paryatan Suchhom Aarthastraya Mikhang (Village Tourism Viewed from Micro Economics),* The Desaymaru Jhaya, March 16, 1995.

Pradhanang, Surendra Bhakta, *A Preliminary Study on the Prospect of Village Tourism Development in the Makalu-Barun Conservation Area with Special Reference to Tashigaun,* Kathmandu : Kathmandu Research Centre, October 1995.

Pradhanang, Surendra Bhakta, *Eco-tourism Management Plan in and around the Royal Chitwan National Park,* Kathmandu : 1997.

Pradhanang, Surendra Bhakta, *Pheri Ke Hola ?* Kathmandu, 2029.

Pradhanang, Surendra Bhakta, *"Productivity in Tourism Sector"* Current Issue on Productivity, Kathmandu : NPCDC 1999.

Pradhanang, Surendra Bhakta, *Village Tourism Marketing Lead by Cargo Industry in Nepal,* Cargo News, Nepal, Vol.2, No. 7, Oct/Nov,1996.

Pradhanang, Surendra Bhakta, *Village Tourism: Not Meaningless Propaganda but Meaningful Plan,* The Explore Nepal, July 15, 1997.

Sharma, Prayag Raj, *Culture and Tourism,* Kathmandu : ICIMOD, 1995 Sharma, Pitamber, *A Framework for Tourism Carrying Capacity Analysis,* Kathmandu : ICIMOD, 1995

Sharma, Udaya Raj, *"Park People Interactions in Royal Chitwan National Park, Nepal." Unpublished Ph.D. Thesis,* The University of Arizona, 1991.

Sherpa, C. Lamu and Lama, Wendy Brewer, *Langtang Village PRA & Appreciative Inquiry Training/ Exercise for Participatory Eco-tourism Planning,* Kathmandu : Langtang Eco-tourism Project, February 1997.

Shrestha, Suresh K. *Eco-tourism, A tool for Conservation and Local Development, 1997.*

Sunday Despatch, *Dumping Tourists Coming to Nepal,* February 22-28, 1998.

Sherstha, Suresh et.al. *Proceedings of Eco-tourism Management Workshop.* Pokhara : Institute of Forest ITTO Project 103/90 Rev. 1 (F), June, 1995.

SHEAC, Institute of Forest, *The Greenery,* An environmental Journal of SHEAC, Vol. 2, Pokhara : Institute of Forest, 1998.

Singh, A.P, *Himalayan Environment and Tourism,* India : Chaugh Publications, First Edition, 1989.

Shengrila, Royal Nepal Airlines, Inflight Magazine April-June, 1998.

The Nepal Weekly, March 7, 2000.

Touche Ross Management Consultants, Nepal, *Tourism Development Programme, Summary of Draft Final Report,* Kathmandu : Asian Development Bank/Ministry of Tourism, Nepal, December 1989.

The Nepal Samacharpatra, Nepal Ma Banyajantoka Angaharuko Taskar, Baisakh 23, 2057 p.2.

Upadhyaya, G.P. *The Characteristics and Satisfactions of International Visitors to Royal Chitwan National Park, Nepal, Unpublished M.A. thesis,* Lincoln University, Canterbury, New Zealand, 1993.

Warford, Jeremy J, *"Approach to Environment Management : Command and Control vs. Economic Instruments", Background Paper for the Economic Development Institute Seminar on Integrated Development and Planning Approaches in Nepal,* Kathmandu, 16-21 January, 1997.

World Tourism Organisation, *Sustainable Tourism Development; Guide for Local Planners*, Madrid : WTO, 1993.

World Tourism Organisation, *Guidelines : Development of National Parks and Protected Areas for Tourism*, Madrid, WTO, 1992.

A View of the Royal Chitwan National Park

Some Tourists Entring the Royal Chitwan National Park

Village House and Environment

Canoing in Naroyani River

Village Tourism in Favour of Trekking Tourism

A Fisherman (Bhote) is Busy in Fish Catching

Beesh Hazare Lake in Chitwan

Village Based International Tourism Programme : Trans Himalaya 2000 Held in Napal. TAAN-President Mr. Rajendra Bantawa Was Delivering an Inagural Speech in The Occasion

Tharu Village Environment in Chitwan

Reu River Introducing Beach Tourism of Madi Kalyanpur

Bachhanli Village House

Village hut in Chitwan

Crocodile in RCNP

Rhinos in The Royal Chitwan National Park

Rhino in The Jungle

Tourists Coming Back from Sirubar Tourist Village After Receiving Warm Farewell.

Local Tharu Man in Economic Activity

Elephant Service to Tourists in Chitwan

Maghis's Fishing Profession in Chitwan

Tourism in Sauraha

The Tharu Young men Standing for Culture Show

Stick Dance of Tharues

Boating Service in Narayani River

The Tharu Male and Female Wearing ornaments

The Tharu Family in the Village

Ox-Cart, Riding

Handicrafts Displaying in The Tharu Village

Traditional House (hut) of Sirubari Tourist Village